Developing a Loving Pedagogy in the Early Years

Care and caring are key to early childhood education and yet love can be viewed as a taboo word within early childhood settings. This book guides practitioners through the potentially problematic area of loving the children they care for. It shows where a loving pedagogy can fit within professional practice and how this can enrich experiences for children and educators.

The book explores how educators can support their children by holding them in mind, valuing them and promoting their best interests. Focusing on how relationships, attachment and connections underpin our settings and practice, the chapters cover:

- the fundamentals of professional love

- appropriate touch in practice

- the different ways in which children feel loved

- the rights of the child

- empowering children through love

- working with parents and carers.

Including case studies and questions for reflection, this is vital reading for practitioners wanting to develop a nurturing and loving pedagogy that places the child at the centre of their practice.

Tamsin Grimmer is an experienced consultant and trainer, a director of Linden Learning and a senior lecturer in Early Years at Bath Spa University. She is based in Wiltshire, UK.

Developing a Loving Pedagogy in the Early Years

How Love Fits with Professional Practice

Tamsin Grimmer

Routledge
Taylor & Francis Group

LONDON AND NEW YORK

First published 2021
by Routledge
2 Park Square, Milton Park, Abingdon, Oxon OX14 4RN

and by Routledge
52 Vanderbilt Avenue, New York, NY 10017

Routledge is an imprint of the Taylor & Francis Group, an informa business

British Library Cataloguing-in-Publication Data
A catalogue record for this book is available from the British Library

Library of Congress Cataloging-in-Publication Data
Names: Grimmer, Tamsin, author.
Title: Developing a loving pedagogy in the early years:
how love fits with professional practice/Tamsin Grimmer.
Description: Abingdon, Oxon ; New York, NY : Routledge, 2021. |
Includes bibliographical references and index. |
Identifiers: LCCN 2020054011 (print) | LCCN 2020054012 (ebook) |
ISBN 9780367902650 (hardback) | ISBN 9780367902667 (paperback) |
ISBN 9781003023456 (ebook)
Subjects: LCSH: Early childhood education–Psychological aspects. |
Early childhood teachers–Professional relationships. | Love.
Classification: LCC LB1139.23 .G75 2021 (print) |
LCC LB1139.23 (ebook) | DDC 372.21–dc23
LC record available at https://lccn.loc.gov/2020054011
LC ebook record available at https://lccn.loc.gov/2020054012

ISBN: 978-0-367-90265-0 (hbk)
ISBN: 978-0-367-90266-7 (pbk)
ISBN: 978-1-003-02345-6 (ebk)

Typeset in Bembo
by Newgen Publishing UK

This book is dedicated to the staff and children at Widcome Acorns preschool in Bath, without whom my initial MA research would not have been possible. I have changed the names of educators and children to protect their identities, but you know who you are and I am indebted to you for sharing your loving pedagogy with me and inspiring me to go on and write this book. Your children are the lucky ones, they thrive in such a warm and loving environment, thank you.

Contents

Acknowledgements

Firstly, may I thank the team at David Fulton for enabling this book to become a reality by publishing it and helping that side of things run so smoothly. Secondly, huge thanks and respect to Jools Page and her lifetime work researching this area. You inspire so many people, not least me. Thank you for taking the time to read through some of my material, and for giving me advice; it meant such a lot to me.

My family deserve a mention as they not only had to put up with being locked down during a global pandemic but they also had to put up with me hiding away to write this book at the same time! And to my mum, who, yet again, has painstakingly proofread each page, helping me to make this book the best it can be. Thank you.

Lastly, my heartfelt thanks goes to the long list of contributors below. Your professional knowledge, stories, anecdotes, photographs and musings have really brought a loving pedagogy to life and will inspire so many people. Some of you have had in-depth conversations with me and acted like a sounding board or given me wonderful professional insights, while others have shared intimate stories of their adventures with their children. Thank you.

Contributors

Alison Shires, Snapdragons Nurseries

Aneesa Jangharia, Sunning Hill Primary School

Bath Spa University Students: Charlotte, Francesco, Hannah, Hazel, Joshua, Lorna, Marlis, Reuben, Summer, Verity

Charlotte Adcock, Westview Day Nursery

Chloe Webster, Pebbles Childcare

College Green Nursery School

David Wright, Paintpots Nurseries

Declan Nigel Dowkes, student researcher at the Huddersfield Centre for Research in Education and Society (HudCRES)

Elaine Brown, childminder

Hazel Adamson, Lechlade Little Learners

Jamel Carly Campbell

Julie Denton

Katherine Bate, Cinnamon Brow School Nursery

Kingscliffe Day Nursery

Laura Wall, Choo Choo's Nursery

Lisa Gibbons, Denmead Infant School

Liz Clarke

Lucy Evershed, Bluecoat Nursery

Lucy Waterman, Love Early Years

Marlis Juerging-Coles, St John's Preschool

Milford Lodge, Australia

North Bradley Primary School

Paula Lochrie

Rebecca Brooks

Sally Kirkby, Headington Quarry Foundation Stage School

Sarah Scott, Dandelions Day Nursery

Sonia Maidstone-Cotton

Sue Searson

Tracy, Feniton Church of England Primary School

Verity Ash, Judy's House Nursery

Widcome Acorns, Bath

Introduction

Several years ago, I came across a journal article written by Page based on her PhD research. Page (2011) posed the question: Do mothers want professional carers to love their babies? This idea ignited something in me and I found myself thinking more and more about the topic and reflecting upon the themes discussed. I had recently become a mother for the first time and so this particularly resonated with me. I found myself reflecting on whether I would want my daughter's educators to 'love' her? For me, it was, and remains, a resounding yes! In fact, if my children's educators don't love my children in a professional context I would feel quite put out! Why not? What's so wrong with my children that you can't love them?!

I also began to reflect upon my feelings as an educator myself. I had previously taught young children in schools but was then working as a childminder, which allows for an even closer relationship. I can honestly say that I had a very deep sense of care and affection for the children I looked after. Would I go so far as to call it love? Most definitely, I loved them. I would have been devastated if anything happened to any of them and found that I felt a real sense of loss when they left my class or setting. Was it the same as the love I feel for my own children? Of course not, but that doesn't make it any less real or less loving.

In addition to these thoughts around loving the children I cared for, I was also exploring the love I have for my own children as a mother and read a book aimed at parents about love languages (Chapman and Campbell, 2012). This links beautifully with attunement and suggests that children (we all in fact) have different ways that we like to give and receive love and if we can better understand the children in our care we can enable them to feel more loved. I was reminded of an advert I saw in the past near St. Valentine's Day which went something like, 'Nothing says "I love you" like red roses …' For some people these roses may well be received as a statement of undying love; however, another person may say this is too extravagant and they would rather their loved one spent time with them, or if their loved one helped them with cleaning the house that would be a more meaningful expression of love. I explore this concept further in Chapter 5. However, these ideas, alongside the interest in love that Page had sparked in me, spurred me on to research this area further.

As an early childhood educator, reading around these two ideas pieced together other thoughts I had been exploring about listening to young children, following a child-centred approach and supporting children's emotional wellbeing and development. It was as if, in the context of love, all these ideas knitted together into a beautiful tapestry! I wondered how children experience feeling loved in their early childhood settings and this led me to study again, so I completed a Master's Degree to look into this, my dissertation title being, *Is there a place for love in an early childhood setting?* Through talking to educators and observing children, I researched how love actually unfolds in a setting and what it looked like in practice. This book draws upon this research, other research, theory and literature from academics and includes stories, anecdotes and case-

studies that I have gathered over a number of years.

I strongly believe that children should grow up in a society where they are loved and this needs to continue within their early childhood settings and schools. If educators love the children in their care and understand how they prefer to be loved, they will better understand how to relate to them and will do so more appropriately, which, in turn, will enable the children to learn more effectively. Therefore I have written this book to encourage educators to adopt a loving pedagogy from the outset so that it underpins all policy and practice within their setting. I feel passionately that loving relationships should be celebrated within our settings and not glossed over or kept as a taboo subject. I want to inspire educators to love, talk about love and be bold when it comes to enhancing their pedagogy through love.

Pedagogy

At this point I should probably unpick the term 'pedagogy'. It comes from the Greek 'paidagogeo' and means to lead the child. I like the thought of leading a child, but not in an authoritative manner, more in a gentle way that scaffolds their learning, presents them with opportunities and a stimulating and enabling learning environment. It reminds me of this picture of my mum and my youngest daughter Becky, taken at the beach. Becky is walking slightly ahead of Granny, leading her to where she wants to go. Granny is loosely holding her hand, enough to guide her if she needs it, but loose enough to allow Becky the freedom to go in her own direction.

The term pedagogy tends to be used to mean the philosophy or approach underpinning the instruction of teachers (Beckley, 2012) and the Researching Effective Pedagogy in the Early Years Project (Siraj-Blatchford et al., 2002: 27) explains:

> Pedagogy is often referred to as the practice (or the art, the science or the craft) of teaching but in the early years any adequate conception of educative practice must be wide enough to include the provision of learning environments for play and exploration.

So within the context of early childhood I think we need to view the term broadly and consider teaching as the practice of educators. By using the phrase a loving pedagogy I aim to combine the caring aspects of our role and describe an approach to working with children that can underpin all aspects of our provision.

To love and feel loved

Maslow (2013) includes to love and be loved as a basic desire to be satisfied in his hierarchy of human needs and most people would agree that loving and feeling loved are very important aspects of their lives. Indeed, people seek out social interaction from birth and developing relationships from our earliest days is vitally important. Despite most people accepting love as a basic human need, love is rarely talked about within early childhood settings. However, children's wellbeing is high on the social and political agenda within England so the time is ripe to talk about love openly and consider how we can develop a loving pedagogy and then put these ideas into action.

Liao argues that children have a right to be loved and that, "Being loved is a condition that is primary essential for children to have a good life" (Liao, 2006: 422). He explains that love provides children the opportunity to trust in others and trust in themselves and gives them examples of how to love and the motivation to accept and obey the demands placed upon them by their loved one, predominately their parent. These, he argues, are reason enough for others to accept children's right to be loved. However, thinking in terms of rights becomes complicated when we think about a concept like love. This is because using the language of rights could imply duty and if I am loving through duty, is it really love? Who carries out this duty? Is the duty placed on parents, carers, educators or society as a whole? Chapters 1 and 6 pick up on the idea of duty in different contexts. I do not claim to have all the answers, however, I want to begin a dialogue about love and its place within early childhood.

Attachment

There is a wealth of research that outlines the importance of developing secure attachments, and research has shown that developing secure attachments with main caregivers has a positive impact on children's lives (Bowlby, 1953; Elfer, 2011). Chapter 8 explores this in a little more detail. Within early childhood settings we have established systems that are rooted in attachment theory, for example the key person approach, the idea that each child is assigned an adult who looks out for them in particular and oversees their individual needs, helping them to feel safe, secure and cared for. Of course, I would add loved to this list too!

Safe Haven

The child relies on their carer for comfort when feeling worried

Secure Base

The child has a good solid foundation from which they can explore

Proximity Maintenance

The child prefers to remain close to their main carer

Separation Distress

The child becomes unhappy or distressed when separated from their main carer

Gerhardt (2004) argues that affection, particularly within the first year of a child's life, has a huge impact on their brain development and later lifelong attitudes and dispositions. Although, interestingly, love is rarely mentioned except in the title of her book: *Why Love Matters…*, however, it is implicit throughout and the role of the adult is emphasised. We know that relationships built by caregivers take time to develop and are central to the emotional development of a child (Page, 2013) so we need to invest in developing these relationships and ensuring that they are built on love and affection.

Love in policy

In recent years issues such as intimate relationships, stories relating to childbirth and the sharing of feelings and emotions have moved from the private arena into the public realm and a growing number of publications consider children's wellbeing. However, love is not always mentioned. Page and colleagues have reopened the dialogue about love, although this has yet to impact on policy and within the context of early childhood, love is seldom referred to in policy documents (Page, 2014).

The term loving has actually been removed from policy within England! In the Practice Guidance for the Early Years Foundation Stage the principle relating to positive relationships originally read: "Children learn to be strong and independent from a base of loving and secure relationships with parents and/or a key person" (DfCSF, 2008: 5). When it was revised in 2012, the wording was shortened and the reference to love removed. This remained the same in subsequent revisions and love has not made it into the revised 2020 document either. In addition, the original Practice Guidance for the Early Years Foundation Stage also referred to "warm and loving relationships" when discussing children as skilful communicators (DfCSF, 2008: 41). Again, this wording was removed when it was revised. However, Early Education (2012: 2) sought to maintain the presence of love within English policy by retaining the broad definition of positive relationships as being "warm and loving" in their non-statutory guidance document, thus keeping the terminology alive within practice. I was really pleased to see that the new revised version of *Development Matters* references love. It states: "Babies, toddlers and young children thrive when they are loved and well cared for" (DfE, 2020: 5), and: "When settling a baby or toddler into nursery, the top priority is for the key person to develop a strong and loving relationship with the young child" (DfE, 2020: 26).

When researching this, I found that there is generally very little written about love in early childhood policy. However some countries talk more openly about love than others. For example, in Hungary unmeasurable qualities such as love are valued and regarded as important. However, a study that compared English and Hungarian pedagogy found that love was diminishing from policy in both countries (Campbell-Barr, Georgeson and Varga, 2015). Theorists from Finland have been discussing pedagogical love for over 150 years (Määttä and Uusiautti, 2012). And recently love and care have been discussed as being included within the educators' role in the Australian Early Childhood Education and Care sector (Rouse and Hadley, 2018). Such studies indicate

that love can be freely discussed within the context of early childhood and it needs to be reinstated within policy. I believe that the time is ripe for us to open a dialogic discussion about pedagogical love and for it to be placed securely within policy as well as lived out in practice.

Despite rarely being seen within international policy, love is regularly discussed with young children, for example, in relation to our families, special people or even Valentine's Day. There are numerous picture books specifically about love and special relationships and many fairy tales depict loving scenes. However, I believe that the lack of references to love and loving relationships in policy and curriculum documents devalues love and lowers its profile within an early childhood context. Further research is needed in this area to help to promote the cause but, thanks to Page and her colleagues, the conversation has started.

Perhaps the reason why love is absent from policy is not a deliberate attempt to water down the strength of feeling, but instead could be linked to the cultural use of the word 'love'. Historically, the term love has not been used in an educational context. This omission could simply be linked to a popular understanding of love and the way that it is inextricably linked to sexual desire and intimacy, which would be inappropriate in an educational setting. These ideas are discussed in more detail in Chapters 1 and 2.

The benefits of a loving pedagogy

The main benefit to adopting a loving pedagogy is that children will feel loved, and have a sense of belonging and will want to be part of our setting and spend time in our company. The ethos will give children the message that it's OK to be you here. We love you for being *you* and we want to help you grow to be the best *you* you can be! So children will feel accepted just as they are, and loved for being themselves. This in turn will raise levels of wellbeing and children's self-esteem. I also think that adopting a loving pedagogy helps to foster positive dispositions to learning, such as the characteristics of effective learning, and also helps to build really strong and secure relationships with both children and their families.

A loving pedagogy firmly places the child at the centre of our practice. Young children spend a vast amount of time within early childhood settings, often a larger proportion of their waking lives than at home. Therefore it is vital that children feel loved and accepted during their time with us.

Developing a loving pedagogy is important because it:

- empowers the children, offers them advocacy and a voice – by being sensitive to their needs, holding them in mind, listening to them, wanting the best for them;

- offers the children a loving environment within which they can thrive;

- gives permission for educators to act and talk in naturally loving ways;

- reiterates to parents that we care very deeply about their children, so it can reassure them that they are well looked after and happy;

- makes our setting a happier place and adults and children alike have a higher wellbeing;

- positively impacts children's lives and keeps them at the heart of everything we do.

Outline of book

For the purposes of this book I use the term 'settings' very broadly to encompass all schools, private, voluntary and independent settings and childminding establishments. I am using the term 'educator' to include all adults who work alongside children regardless of their level of qualification or experience. When I refer to 'parents' I do so broadly, not only referring to birth-parents but also the main carers of a child, for example foster carers, grandparents or step-parents.

I have gathered stories, anecdotes and case studies from colleagues, parents and early years educators who have developed a loving pedagogy in their own settings or have an interest in this area. I have mostly used a pseudonym for the children unless a parent has given me specific permission to use their real name. Wherever possible, children have also been consulted about use of any case study material or photographs. I have attempted to consider representation, for example, in terms of background or type of setting to try to ensure that this book contains not only my own viewpoint but shares the perspective of others. I have also consulted and discussed what a loving pedagogy might look like with hundreds of early years educators from a variety of different settings around the UK as I have been delivering training or through my own teaching at Bath Spa University.

This book is divided into different chapters, which each pick up on a theme which I have linked to a loving pedagogy. I have included a few case studies and photographs to further illustrate and bring to life the themes covered. Each chapter concludes with some questions designed to enable you to reflect upon your practice in the light of what you have read. These questions should facilitate you to explore the issues raised in each chapter and further develop your practice.

Chapter 1 shares different definitions of love and considers what we might include in a definition within an educational context, particularly within early childhood. It will look at practical examples of the various definitions and share a little about the research that has been completed in this field.

Chapter 2 explores why educators may not want to talk about love and covers issues such as whether parents want us to love their children and if love is an appropriate term to use in early childhood. It also addresses the problems relating to the intimacy of love, including child protection and safeguarding concerns.

Chapter 3 focuses on what I mean when I refer to the term professionalism and how I believe it can be applied to the context of love in early years. It links with Page's work around 'professional love' (2018, 2014, 2011) and considers the complex nature of loving children in professional roles. It will also raise the debate around how others can sometimes view early childhood educators as babysitters or an extension of mothers verses true professionals.

Chapter 4 addresses the tactile nature of a loving pedagogy and reflects upon the hands-on aspects of early childhood education. It will look at research that discusses the importance of touch in children's lives and will also consider what constitutes appropriate and/or positive touch in practice.

Chapter 5 draws upon Chapman and Campbell's work (2012) on love languages. They outline five ways that we might prefer or choose to give and receive love and how important it is to speak our children's (love) language. It will also consider how we can use this approach within early childhood settings to support children.

Chapter 6 looks at issues relating to the rights of the child (Unicef, 1989), how we can listen to children through our interactions with them and the balance of power in adult–child relationships. It will consider the ways in which developing a loving pedagogy in our settings can empower our children.

Chapter 7 draws upon Read's idea of 'holding children in mind' and links it with mind-mindedness (Meins, 1997) and attunement. It will also consider ideas around how our ethos and learning environment can support a loving pedagogy. Lastly, it will share practical ideas of how we can hold children in mind in our settings.

Chapter 8 discusses loving relationships in terms of working with parents and carers, the children themselves and between children. It considers how relationships, attachment and connections underpin our settings and practice. It also makes links between our relationship with the setting and the attachment we feel to the space, in addition to the people.

Chapter 9 concludes by drawing together the various themes within the book and presenting practical ideas of how we can develop a loving pedagogy in practice. It summarises the learning from the different chapters and offers ideas of where to take this next and how the conversation can continue. Hopefully it will inspire educators to love, talk about love and be bold!

As I began writing this book, the world faced the coronavirus pandemic and therefore I have included an afterword. I have entitled it 'demonstrating a loving pedagogy during a pandemic' because, for me, in many settings, this difficult time was evidence of a loving pedagogy in practice. Settings had to literally live out their ethos, and came up with beautiful, creative ways of caring for, supporting and loving their children.

References

Beckley, P. (2012). *Learning in Early Childhood: A Whole Child Approach from birth to 8*. London: Sage.

Bowlby, J. (1953). *Childcare and the Growth of Love*. London: Penguin books.

Campbell-Barr, V., Georgeson, J. and Varga, A. (2015). Developing professional early childhood educators in England and Hungary: Where has all the love gone? *European Education, 47*, 311–330.

Chapman, G. and Campbell, R. (2012). *The 5 Love Languages of Children*. Chicago, IL: Northfield Publishing.

Department for Children, Schools and Families (DfCSF) (2008). *Statutory Framework for the Early Years Foundation Stage, Practice Guidance*. London: Department for Children, Schools and Families.

Department for Education (DfE) (2020). *Development Matters: Non-statutory Curriculum Guidance for the Early Years Foundation Stage*. Retrieved from https://foundationyears.org.uk/2020/09/new-development-matters-published/.

Early Education (2012). *Development Matters in the Early Years Foundation Stage*. London: Early Education. Retrieved from www.early-education.org.uk/development-matters.

Elfer, P. (2011). *Key Persons in Early Years Settings and Primary Schools*. London: Routledge.

Gerhardt, S. (2004). *Why Love Matters: How Affection Shapes a Baby's Brain*. Hove: Brunner-Routledge.

Liao, M. (2006). The right of children to be loved. *The Journal of Political Philosophy, 14*(4), 420–440.

Määttä, K. and Uusiautti, S. (2012). Pedagogical authority and pedagogical love – connected or incompatible? *International Journal of Whole Schooling, 8*(1), 21–33.

Maslow, A. (2013). *A Theory of Human Motivation*. Radford, VA: Wilder Publications.

Meins, E. (1997). *Security of Attachment and the Social Development of Cognition*. Hove: Psychology Press.

Page, J. (2011). Do mothers want professional carers to love their babies? *Journal of Early Childhood Research, 9*(3) 310–323.

Page, J. (2013). Permission to love them. In J. Page, A. Clare and C. Nutbrown (eds.), *Working with Babies and Young Children from Birth to Three*. London: Sage.Page, J. (2014). Developing 'professional love' in early childhood settings. In L. Harrison and J. Sumsion (eds.), *Lived Spaces of Infant–Toddler Education and Care – Exploring Diverse Perspectives on Theory, Research, Practice and Policy*. Vol 11. International Perspectives on Early Childhood Education and Development Series. London: Springer Publishing (pp 119–130).

Page, J. (2018). Characterising the principles of professional love in early childhood care and education. *International Journal of Early Years Education, 26*(2), 125–141.Rouse, E. and Hadley, F. (2018). Where did love and care get lost? Educators and parents' perceptions of early childhood practice. *International Journal of Early Years Education, 26*(2), 159–172.

Siraj-Blatchford, I., Sylva, K., Muttock, S., Gilden, R. and Bell, D. (2002). *Researching Effective Pedagogy in the Early Years*. Retrieved from https://dera.ioe.ac.uk/4650/1/RR356.pdf.

Unicef (1989). United Nations Convention on the Rights of the Child. Retrieved from www.unicef.org.uk/Documents/Publication-pdfs/UNCRC_PRESS200910web.pdf.

1 Defining love

Introduction

The need to be loved can be described as a basic human need (Maslow, 2013). I have found that most professional educators, like me, have very deep feelings for the children in their care. Many would describe this as a sort of professional love. However love is not a term that is synonymous with education and the term is rarely used within early childhood education and care. But what do we actually mean when we use the word 'love' and how can we relate this to an educational context? This chapter will share various definitions of love and attempt to define it within an early childhood context to clarify what is meant when the term is used. It will look at practical examples of these definitions and share a little about the research that has been completed in this field.

Defining love

Defining love is not as simple as it sounds. Love is an abstract concept. It is not easily defined and yet is so full of meaning and depth. Love means different things in different contexts. You can love in various ways and perhaps to a greater or lesser extent. For example, I love my mum very differently to how I love my husband and I love my own children differently to how I have loved children I have cared for as a childminder or teacher. But I would still call it love. In many languages there are a variety of words to sum up these meanings. However in English there is one word to encompass all these subtly different circumstances, which can be problematic because they mean such different things and some could be described as morally inappropriate in relation to children.

Love is a word that could be viewed as 'out of bounds' by some early childhood educators. This could be because of a popular understanding of love which inextricably links it to sexual desire and intimacy (Aslanian, 2018; Cousins, 2017). Defining love in this way would be inappropriate within the context of early childhood education and understandably makes some educators wary of using the term. However, love is not confined to the romantic notion of lovers. It is also a word that we use within the context of family and friends, nature and even our favourite foods. As educators we need to reclaim the word 'love' and 'loving pedagogy' and use them appropriately in our settings to describe our intense feelings and our ethos that underpins our practice.

What do we mean when we talk of love? A deep feeling, or a desire to want the best for someone? It is interesting that when we talk to people about love and what they mean by the word, we might get very different answers depending on age, culture, languages spoken and so on. For example, I would suggest that love is not simply a feeling or an emotion; it is much more about deliberate actions, like acting in the best interests of someone else, looking out for them and enjoying spending time together. Whereas someone else might suggest that love is about attraction or passion and definitely about the way you feel.

The *Collins Online Dictionary* defines the verb 'to love' as involving more than just emotions: "You say that you love someone when their happiness is very important to you, so that you behave in a kind and caring way towards them" (Collins Online Dictionary, 2020). Generally speaking, it is accepted that loving others also involves a certain etiquette or behaviour and this idea is explored more fully in Chapter 7 when I discuss holding children in mind.

Friendship, Westview Day Nursery

We believe that it is really important for children to understand about friendship, which we see as the first stage of love. We encourage children to talk about friends and often play games that encourage social interaction. For example, before lunch we meet together as a group and often sing songs together. During this song one child chooses a friend to dance with at the end of each verse. We often find that children might not initially want to dance but choose to when invited by their friends.

While I was researching how to define love in an educational context, I came across an article written for *SecEd*, a magazine and website that supports secondary teachers in the UK. The author describes how, after beginning a new headship in a secondary school, he asked his team about what we mean as parents when we state we love our children. He suggested that, "We mean that we are committed to caring for and protecting our children. We will treat our children as individuals, with different needs and expectations. We will put their interests before our own" (Wood, 2013: 1). He goes on to say that the teacher's role and parent's role are practically identical in this desire.

This definition talks about our commitment to care and protect, cater for individual needs and the necessity to 'put their interests before our own'. This self-less notion often typifies love in a romantic sense: 'Do you love someone enough to give them your last Rolo?' springs to mind! But also, on a more serious note, it is this self-less love that defines parental love, when pushed to extremes, if you think about families who are starving and a parent who gives their child the last morsel of food they have. Putting other people first does not necessarily fit with many of the ideas within contemporary society, where we are invited to view ourselves as having a right to look after our own interests and put ourselves first. Despite this, most educators would agree that a loving pedagogy keeps the child in the centre and thus promotes their needs above our own.

The characteristics of love

When we think about defining love, we sometimes think about the different characteristics of love or the manifestations of love. When someone loves someone else, how do they act or which actions typify their behaviour? People may think of religious texts, and one that is very widely known and regularly read at marriage ceremonies is a passage from the Bible, the collection of writings that Christians refer to as their scripture. In one of the best definitions of love that I have read, it states:

> Love is patient, love is kind. It does not envy, it does not boast, it is not proud. It does not dishonour others, it is not self-seeking, it is not easily angered, it keeps no record of wrongs. Love does not delight in evil but rejoices with the truth. It always protects, always trusts, always hopes, always perseveres. Love never fails.
>
> (1 Corinthians 13: 4–8, Holy Bible, 2011)

Although this passage is relating to love in the context of a loving God, I feel that it can be useful in helping us to unpick the different characteristics of love in terms of our relationship with the children. In this table I have taken each adjective or phrase and attempted to find examples from practice of when we see this in action.

Love statement	Example from practice
Love is patient	We try to be patient with the children, for example when we know that it will take longer for them to put on their own wellies than if we help them, but we wait and let them do it for themselves.
Love is kind	When we seek out a specific toy that we know a particular child will love or when we plan certain activities with individual children in mind.
Love does not envy	We need to role-model how to react when we feel envious or jealous so that children will learn how to respond appropriately. For example, I talk about really liking my friend's new bag and ask the children, is it OK for me to take the bag because I really want it? So we illustrate that it is understandable to have the feelings of being envious or jealous but we must be careful not to act upon these feelings.
Love does not boast	We would not dream of saying we are better than the children or we know more than one of our colleagues. Acting in a loving way is not being boastful or thinking of ourselves as better than others.
Love is not proud	This is not about celebrating achievements – we should teach children to take pride in what they do. This is actually referring to self-pride and being arrogant or being unable to admit that we are wrong. Acting in a loving way would be telling the children when we have made a mistake and explaining why we would do things differently another time.
Love does not dishonour others	This refers to having good manners, being respectful and not being rude to other people. Again, we role model this to our children.
Love is not self-seeking	We do not seek our own fulfilment but instead we put the children's needs first, selflessness. Love is also not demanding our own way but allowing others to lead and make their own choices too, even when they are different from ours.
Love is not easily angered	This is when we take a deep breath, repeat an instruction for the nth time and still remain calm. Also when we are working with children we do not take offence at the things they say because we know that they are young and may not fully understand what they are saying.
Love keeps no record of wrongs	When every day in our setting is a clean sheet and we do not talk to the children in terms of past behaviour, instead we focus on the present and future.
Love does not delight in evil but rejoices with the truth	If one child told another that they were stupid, we would remind them to only use kind words. But we would not leave it there. We would build up the hurt child's self-esteem by reminding them of the things they are good at, and countering the unkind words with kind, truthful words.

Love statement	Example from practice
Love always protects	Safeguarding is our primary concern in settings, we always protect our children to the best of our ability. We also create safe spaces in our environment to help children to feel secure.
Love always trusts	We should think about children as competent learners. We also build trusting relationships where the children have confidence in us and feel safe physically and emotionally.
Love always hopes	When we look for the good in our children and always want them to reach their potential.
Love always perseveres	We do not give up on our children. We want the best for them and will fight their corner should it be necessary.
Love never fails	This is about our unconditional love, which endures through every circumstance regardless of the child's behaviour or interactions with us.

Love according to the ancient Greeks

Love is a complex word and, as mentioned earlier, languages other than English tend to use different words to describe its very different aspects. The most famous is probably the ancient Greeks who had many different words to describe love, for example *agápe*, *éros*, *philía*, *philautia*, *storgē*, *xenia*, *ludus* and *pragma*.

Agápe is usually used to describe the love of God for humankind, God's faithfulness and commitment to humans. It often relates to sacrifice. *Agápe* is about unconditional and compassionate love, which is self-less and wanting the best or the greatest good for the other person. Charity would also come under this heading. From everything that I have read, the world needs more of this type of love!

The term *éros* refers to erotic, sexual love. Think romance and passion. This is not a type of love that we would refer to in relation to children. *Philía* is about platonic love, or the attraction within friendship. This is where people bond over similar or shared interests and depend and trust each other. It would also be used to describe companionship and brotherly love.

Philautia refers to self-love which can be healthy or unhealthy – unhealthy if you place yourself above all others and healthy if through loving yourself you learn about how to love others. Perhaps you can only fully love and accept others if you love and accept yourself. The term *storgē* is used to describe affection or familial love. Think about the medieval proverb 'blood is thicker than water' or the idea that family love is powerful and often associated with dependency. So *storgē* would be the love that parents naturally feel for their children, a love that requires very little effort and enables us to forgive and accept each other and make sacrifices if necessary. This love helps children to feel secure, comfortable and safe. I wonder if it is *storgē* that we also naturally feel for our children in our care, or whether it is too simplistic to suggest that this can be replicated outside of the family.

Xenia refers to the sort of love that incorporates hospitality, generosity, respect and courtesy. It could be argued that this is not necessarily love. However, it is usually included in any lists that you read about the Greek words for love. In one sense, in offering our children hospitality in our settings and through being respectful and courteous we are demonstrating this type of love. When considering developing a loving pedagogy in a holistic way, including *xenia* makes sense.

Ludus refers to playful love which is uncommitted and flirtatious. It is the fun kind of love that in today's language would imply a no-strings-attached relationship. It can be linked to sexual desire and attraction and thus would not be appropriate to consider in terms of the child-like play that we lovingly engage in within our settings.

Lastly, *pragma* describes the practical love founded on reason or duty and one's longer term interests and shared goals. Chapter 6 explores the idea of duty a little further when it considers unconditional love. *Pragma* is in direct contrast to *ludus* as it is about a long-standing love that has endured over time. Although this type of love does not focus on sexual desire, it usually refers to the staying in love part of long-term romantic relationships.

It is helpful to unpick these different terms when thinking about our settings, *agápe*, *philia*, *storgē*, *xenia* and, to a certain extent, *pragma* are all the types of love that may be relevant to us as educators. They describe different aspects of how we might love the children in our care and have been explored in the table.

Type of love	Example from practice
Agápe	Our love does not depend on the children's behaviour; it is unconditional. We genuinely want the best or the greatest good for the children in our care.
Philia	We build up attachments with children that are strengthened through shared interests and experiences. Our children depend on and trust us and we encourage children to build strong friendships with both educators and their peers.
Storgē	We are acting *in loco parentis*, protecting children and helping them to feel safe and secure. Many settings are described as an extended family, and many educators naturally feel love for the children in their care.
Xenia	We offer our children hospitality in our settings, by feeding them and providing a safe, stimulating and engaging learning environment. We ensure that we respect others and role model being kind and caring behaviours.
Pragma	We have a practical duty to safeguard children and protect them and ensure that our environment is safe and secure. Also, putting risk assessments in place is an example of pragma in action.

Love in different cultures

Some cultures will demonstrate love through touch and very public displays of affection, while others will be more reserved but still love as abundantly. It is important for early childhood educators to bear in mind cultural differences when we think about love and try to avoid making assumptions due to the way children may interact lovingly with each other or refrain from this in public. This being said:

> Love is a universal emotion experienced by a majority of people, in various historical eras, and in all the world's cultures, but manifests itself in different ways because culture has an impact on people's conceptions of love and the way they feel, think, and behave.
>
> (Karandashev, 2015: 1)

It must be noted that this quote is primarily in relation to romantic love. However, it can be agreed that cultural values and traditions have a profound impact on the way that love is experienced and the way that people in love behave. So, although we find evidence of love in all cultures, the way love is expressed may differ. This idea links closely with my interpretation of love languages when we all have different ways that we prefer to give and receive love and is discussed in more detail in Chapter 5.

In discussion with Jamel Carly Campbell

I interviewed Jamel prior to writing this book and he pointed out the importance of considering what love looks like from different cultures when defining love. He reminisced about his relationship with his grandmother, who, like some Jamaicans, are not 'touchy-feely'. Instead, she demonstrated her love through cooking for them or through praising their achievements and talking about them to her friends. Even though she may not have shown affection through constantly hugging or touch, he was left in no doubt about her love for him.

There are also cultural differences about the extent to which people associate emotions and an emotional connection with love. In some cultures, loving someone requires a huge emotional investment, whereas in others emotions rarely come into it. We may see these differences in our settings by the way that children appear attached or detached to others emotionally. Some children might respond in a very emotional way to instruction, while others may respond in a more passive or apathetic way where they could appear uncaring. This might not be true, however, and we must ensure that we do not make assumptions based on our own emotional interpretation of a child's response.

Children learn to express their emotions in the same way that they learn many skills, by imitation, and if they are living in a home where culturally, feelings tend to be repressed, they are less likely to show emotion in our settings.

Another interesting point in relation to culture is that, when comparing people who were passionately in love, research using MRI scans found that the brain activity was very similar in people from different cultures. They also found that patterns of brain activity were almost identical when comparing both passionate love and maternal love (Karandashev, 2015). Interestingly, the parts of the brain with most activity were the more primitive parts of the brain, which suppress the areas responsible for critical thought, implying that love is a primeval response and one that the survival of our species depends upon. This makes sense when you think of it in terms of mating or procreation. Passionate love is all about the survival of our species and having babies! This also accounts for the depth of feeling involved when we think about love. If our survival depends upon it, we are not going to take it lightly.

A preschool's story, London

Our setting is in a very ethnically diverse catchment area and many children do not speak English when they arrive. Although we are a small setting, our children and families speak over ten languages. Many of these families are refugees and have not been living in London for long. We have found that these families need more support and our loving pedagogy has really helped us in doing this. We have also found that having this pedagogy helps us to value families and demonstrate respect and understanding. Our staff team is also diverse, speaking many languages, which helps. However, we also use lots of pictures, gestures and signs to help us to communicate. We have built a very inclusive environment and ethos, where all members of staff and families are encouraged to fully participate and cooperate in the life of the setting.

I believe that building on a foundation of a loving pedagogy is the most inclusive approach we can adopt because love has no culture, no colour, no race, no gender, no ability or inability. You could say that love knows no bounds. Instead, love provides us with a basic instinct to protect and care for others.

The terminology of love

Love is a term that more and more educators are referring to and there is currently a resurgence of research into love within early childhood settings, much of which is due to Page and her colleagues and their valuable contribution to research (2018, 2014). Cousins (2017: 17) defines love, for the purposes of her research with early childhood educators, as "to have and express, or show, affection for someone. This feeling and expression of affection, or love, may be intense. It may contain warmth, fondness and high regard for another person." Another definition that resonates with me is the concept of holding children in mind (Read, 2014). This is when we keep the child at the centre of our provision, plan with them in mind and this for me describes putting love into action, helping to keep love as more active and less based on feeling.

Despite love being more freely discussed, many authors allude to love through inference or using alternative words such as 'care', 'warmth' and 'attachment', which Page argues are different, although equally important (2014). Using other terms as euphemisms for love could prove to be unhelpful as they could dilute the depth of emotion and feeling involved. For example, using the word 'warmth' does not explicitly state the intensity of feeling that love implies. Page (2018: 124) refers to the "pseudonymisation of love", which she believes waters down meaning and could restrict and sterilise love in practice.

Gerhardt's famous book, *Why Love Matters* (2004) considers the role that affection has on a child. However, despite the title implying otherwise, love is not explicitly discussed. Dowling (2014: 7) is more specific as she includes a loving response as part of the practitioner's role when she describes a baby being, "ready to reciprocate and flourish in our loving care." Terms such as 'loving relationships', 'care' and 'affection' are embedded within her work, which implies that these values underpin her ethos.

We also tend to think about attachment when we think about loving relationships. However, Bowlby, who could be described as the godfather of attachment, rarely mentions love in his work. It could be argued that their titles alone imply that both

Gerhardt (2004) and Bowlby (1953) consider love to be implicit throughout their writing. However, perhaps they were concerned about the way the word love could be interpreted in their work. This idea is confirmed by Bowlby's son in a lecture that I listened to where he explains that love was dropped from his father's theory. He states:

> My father's first book … was called, Child care and the growth of love …. Love was what my father was talking about, but he was a psychoanalyst as well as a psychiatrist and a medical doctor and he wasn't talking about sex because the Freudian's had sexualised the word love and he had to drop it … Attachment, it's just a word, but it's a word that actually means love.
>
> (Bowlby, 2014: 0:44–1:56)

However, I disagree with this last statement, and have also read some research that would contest this point (Cowden, 2012; Prior and Glaser, 2006). I do not think that attachment means the same thing as love. I believe that a loving pedagogy would usually include attachment and the caregiver bonds that spring to mind when thinking about this. Yet I think a loving pedagogy can encompass more than this and, sadly, having a strong attachment might not always include love. Despite this, there is considerable overlap between care, attachment and love and they would look very similar in practice.

Alison Shires, Snapdragons Nurseries

The senior leadership team at Snapdragons have discussed the use of the word love and thought about how to respond to children if a child says "I love you" to a member of staff. Snapdragon's Nurseries are happy to use the word love although they believe that staff have to feel comfortable in their response so have invited staff to come up with their own ideas of what to say in response, for example: "Thank you", "I love you too" or "What a lovely thing to say!" They also talk about love to the children and sometimes plan activities around love, so that children can think about it in different ways.

Loving interactions

Although it can be difficult to define love, it would be fair to say that we can recognise a loving pedagogy when we see it in practice. Ida (2017) refers to several pieces of research that consider love and a loving demeanour to be an important element of what makes a good teacher. I believe that through studying relationships and interactions, love can also be observed and this was the focus of my Master's thesis. The aim of my study was to paint as true a picture as possible of what love looked like in a pre-school setting and to illuminate how love shines through the practices observed. Through sharing observations of adult–child interactions and having intimate conversations with educators, I outlined how a loving pedagogy exists within day-to-day practices. From dealing sensitively with an accident to cuddling up during carpet time, the adults observed were putting into practice their ideologies and beliefs about how best to care for children. I interpreted these through the lens of love and concluded that such interactions demonstrate a loving pedagogy.

Dylan's story, Widcombe Acorns

Dylan had wet himself and sought out his key person, Heidi. She crouched down next to Dylan and talked quietly to him before standing up and, hand in hand, walked with Dylan to the bathroom, which is just situated through a door off the main playroom. As Heidi left the room she gestured to her colleague Lucy that she was going to the bathroom by pointing to the bathroom and to Dylan. She asked Lucy to collect Dylan's bag, without explaining why it was needed and Lucy understood the inference. Lucy immediately walked to the pegs and collected Dylan's bag, taking it to the bathroom, handed it quietly to Heidi, who thanked Lucy. Dylan reappeared in the play room a few minutes later wearing different trousers, smiling and looking happy. He walked over and joined his friend Milo who was playing with small cars on a rug depicting a road scene.

During the intimate conversations, the love and affection that the educators had for the children in their care was evident. They spoke honestly and passionately about their roles and how they worked hard to develop rapport and secure bonds with them, getting to know the children really well in the process. They shared how they enjoyed being in the company of them and how they wanted the best for the children in their care.

Pat and Lucy's story, Widcombe Acorns

This is part of the transcript from my intimate conversations with educators from my Master's dissertation where we discuss the idea of adults and children feeling comfortable together. Pat mentions "being pleased to see them [children] enjoying their company" and "having a laugh with them". Lucy believes that children feel at ease and loved as she states:

We are very friendly and welcoming and we try to engage all the children and get down to their level and I just think it makes them feel at ease and then, you know they can thrive and enjoy their experience when they're here and I think we do build up really good rapport with them and, you know, they all arrive so happily and separate so happily I think you can see that there is that sort of connection and whether it's, you know, they feel loved … I think we do act in a loving way towards them, you know we're like a little community really and they all feel a part of that which is important so I guess in that sense they feel, yeah, they feel very much loved in the setting.

I continue to be particularly interested in what educators think categorises a loving pedagogy and how it can be seen in practice. With this in mind, during training sessions I invite educators to word storm love within the context of early childhood and the below photo is an example of the outcome! The categories that are usually mentioned include the way we interact with children, our ethos and attitudes and practical ideas that demonstrate love.

When thinking about the way we interact with children, educators include:

- building secure attachments and a close bond with the children;

- getting to know the children really well and developing a strong relationship;

- labelling praise and offering encouragement;

- taking an interest in what children are doing and achieving;

- being responsive and responding sensitively;

- showing care and affection through hugs and positive touch.

When considering our ethos and attitude, they tend to think about helping children to feel different ways, for example: valued, appreciated, understood, accepted for who they are, not judged, happy and listened to. Lastly, they also include practical ideas that demonstrate love, such as:

- getting down to the children's level;

- smiling at each other;

- making eye contact;

- using positive body language;

- demonstrating interest in the children and their play;

- planning around children's interests and fascinations;

- offering help and advice;

- noticing when children's emotions change.

Loving relationships

It is vitally important to define love within the context of loving relationships as, outside this context, it would have far less meaning. We get to know children and families really well during their time with us and this begins from their very first meeting with us. If settings have adopted a loving pedagogy I am keen for this to be evident, not only in practice but also in policy.

Paint Pots Nurseries have sought to do this as they have adopted a motto, 'Love, Laughter and Learning'. This underpins all their practice and they believe that the prerequisite needs must be met at each level before progressing upwards. In other words, there can be no learning without love. They seek to have a collective understanding of professional love in their settings and an open and transparent culture.

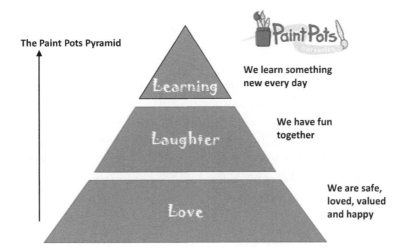

The Paint Pots Pyramid

Learning — We learn something new every day

Laughter — We have fun together

Love — We are safe, loved, valued and happy

This can be really helpful for parents when they are choosing provision for their child, as understanding about the ethos of a setting is really important. Caring for children is a privilege and not something that we should take for granted. Parents are entrusting their most treasured belongings into our care so we need to be open and honest about what we do and why. Elaine describes how she introduces her setting to new families, by sharing her ethos and explaining that her setting is not just a childcare service, it is more of a family.

Elaine Brown: a childminder's story

As a childminder working with young children, I often think back to what was important to me as a child, what helped me feel safe, secure and happy. For me, it always came down to relationships. Being a quiet child, adults that fostered a sense of wellbeing, who made me feel that I really mattered were key to my inner confidence. In my setting, connection is top of my list when it comes to a loving pedagogy. I seek to foster genuine relationships, not only with the children but with their families. In the initial meeting, although I am selling my service, I invest an interest in the parents, I am seeking a connection with these people who are thinking about handing over their most precious gift to someone they have only just met. Parents know more about their child than anyone; that initial and ongoing dialogue is essential to provide that loving ethos for their child. I emphasise that my setting is about family, it is not just a child-care service, we are all on this journey together. I have photographs displayed in my setting of the children in my care, their families, friends, and pets, along with photos of my family, in the hope that this holds a sense of belonging. A safe place, where the parents feel they are a significant part of the childcare path, and their children can also see and feel that the person who cares for them has a true connection and relationship with what is in effect, their 'whole world', their parents and family.

In summary

There are so many definitions of love and so many different ways that we can interpret this term. In this chapter I have shared a few ideas and discussed several definitions, however, for the purposes of this book I am predominantly using Read's (2014) broad idea of 'holding children in mind', which encompasses an adult's nurturing behaviour, thinking about and acting in the best interests of the child and generally caring deeply for them. Unpicking what we mean by love can help us to critically analyse and add depth to our thinking.

Although many educators choose not to use the word 'love' and instead opt for words that are partly synonymous, like 'care' or 'attachment', I believe it to be important to use the word because, in my view, none of the alternatives capture the depth of feeling and the broad nature of love. Therefore, using the term 'loving pedagogy' when describing our ethos helps to embed love and place it securely at the centre of our practice.

Questions for reflection

1. How would you define love in the context of early childhood?

2. Which of the different types of love do you consider to be important in your setting?

3. Can you outline the interactions that make up your own loving pedagogy?

References

Aslanian, T. (2018). Embracing uncertainty: a diffractive approach to love in the context of early childhood education and care. *International Journal of Early Years Education, 26*(2), 173–185.

Bowlby, J. (1953). *Childcare and the Growth of Love.* London: Penguin books.

Bowlby, R. (2014). Lecture on *Attachment Theory – The Science of Love, Part 1.* Presented on November 7, 2014. Video retrieved from www.youtube.com/watch?v=dgaz5NDpBR8.

Collins Online Dictionary (2020). Definition of 'love'. Retrieved from www.collinsdictionary.com/dictionary/english/love.

Cousins, S. (2017). Educators' constructions of love in early childhood education and care. *International Journal of Early Years Education, 25*(1), 16–29.

Cowden, M. (2012). What's love got to do with it? Why a child does not have a right to be loved. *Critical Review of International Social and Political Philosophy, 15*(3), 325–345.

Dowling, M. (2014). *Young Children's Personal, Social and Emotional Development,* 4th edn. London: Sage.

Gerhardt, S. (2004). *Why Love Matters: How Affection Shapes a Baby's Brain.* Hove: Brunner-Routledge.

Holy Bible, New International Version (2011). Retrieved from www.biblegateway.com/passage/?search=1+Corinthians+13%3A4-8&version=NIV.

Ida, Z. (2017). What makes a good teacher? *Universal Journal of Educational Research, 5*(1), 141–147.

Karandashev, V. (2015). A cultural perspective on romantic love. *Online Readings in Psychology and Culture,* 5(4). https://scholarworks.gvsu.edu/cgi/viewcontent.cgi?article=1135&context=orpc.

Maslow, A. (2013). *A Theory of Human Motivation.* Radford, VA: Wilder Publications.

Page, J. (2014). Developing 'professional love' in early childhood settings. In L. Harrison and J. Sumsion (eds.), *Lived Spaces of Infant-Toddler Education and Care – Exploring Diverse Perspectives on Theory, Research, Practice and Policy.* Vol 11. International Perspectives on Early Childhood Education and Development Series. London,: Springer Publishing (pp. 119–130).

Page, J. (2018). Characterising the principles of professional love in early childhood care and education. *International Journal of Early Years Education, 26*(2), 125–141.

Prior, V. and Glaser, D. (2006). *Understanding Attachment and Attachment Disorders: Theory, Evidence and Practice (Child and Adolescent Mental Health).* London: Jessica Kingsley Publishers.

Read, V. (2014). *Developing Attachment in Early Years Settings: Nurturing Secure Relationships from Birth to Five Years,* 2nd edn. Abingdon: Routledge.

Wood, A. (2013). Is professional 'love' appropriate? *SecEd blog,* 12 September. Retrieved from www.sec-ed.co.uk/blog/is-professional-love-appropriate/.

2 Problematising love

Introduction

When I share with other people, outside of education, that I am writing a book about developing a loving pedagogy, most of them respond, "How lovely to write about love!" while those within secondary education tend to reply, "Love? Really? I don't think I'd use that word in relation to my teaching ..." My early childhood colleagues seem to be more on my wavelength and respond, "Ah, that describes what we do in our setting!" A loving pedagogy is not about lovely cosy feelings where everything is smelling of roses. It is actually a difficult concept, with lots of associated problems that this chapter attempts to explore.

Often people will desire to feel loved and will strive to make themselves more 'love-able' by changing their appearance, wearing certain things, making more money, even by taking up a hobby or reading a certain book: "Most people see the problem of love primarily as that of being loved, rather than that of loving, of one's capacity to love. Hence the problem to them is how to be loved, how to be lovable" (Fromm, 2013: 14). This is a typical, yet fairly self-centred, stance to take. According to Fromm: "What most people in our culture mean by being lovable is essentially a mixture between being popular and having sex appeal" (2013: 15). Within early childhood education, the issue is not about making us more lovable, but about loving, our capacity to love the children and the various problems that can result when we go down this road.

Early years educators may not want to use the word 'love', as discussed in Chapter 1. Or some parents may not want educators to love their children. Loving the children can lead to us as educators making some difficult decisions as we want to act in the most loving way, which may require setting boundaries, emotion coaching and problem solving. We can also encounter problems relating to the intimacy of love, including child protection and safeguarding concerns. This chapter will think about these issues and also consider how we can be more trauma and attachment aware in our practice.

Tough love or loving kindness?

Sometimes the most loving thing to do or the most loving way to act is not the easiest. As a parent it would be easy to always give in to all demands; "More sweets? Yes!" "Longer screen time? Of course, darling!" "Do you have to eat your vegetables? No don't worry about it!" But this is not the most loving way to act. If part of acting in a loving way is to want the very best for the person we love, we want them to be healthy and not hurt themselves by their lifestyle and choices. This can mean sometimes not giving in to these demands, despite hearing cries of, "You don't love me anymore!" You have probably heard of 'tough love', when a parent offers warmth but also clear boundaries for their child.

Using the term 'tough love' can itself be problematic because it has often been used in association with other initiatives, like those in sympathy with smacking or a specific parenting style dealing with addiction in the US. I am not referring to these and am using the term more generally to mean when a child is treated with warm affection, but alongside simple rules and boundaries designed to keep the child safe and healthy. A report funded by the Equality and Human Rights Commission found that there are typically four main parenting styles: laissez-faire, authoritarian, disengaged and tough love. They measure these according to the level of warmth/hostility and the degree to which a parent is permissive/controlling. In their study, tough love was the most positive of the four styles and the one that had the greatest impact on children:

> This group of parents combine a warm and responsive approach to child rearing with firm rules and clear boundaries. They are assertive without being aggressive or restrictive and the aim of their disciplinary methods is to reason with and support their child rather than to be punitive. Children from 'tough loving' families are characterised as cooperative, self-regulating and socially responsible.
>
> (Lexmond and Reeves, 2009: 46)

In our settings we need to practise our own version of tough love or, as I prefer to call it, loving kindness, when we make decisions while holding the children in mind and wanting the very best for them. Our response needs to be warm, loving and kind while we still set boundaries to help keep the children safe and protected, so we may not always be responding in the way the child would like as they do not see the bigger picture. We may not be practising this to the same extent as parents, but we still have difficult choices to make at times.

Katie's story: a childminder's perspective

I used to look after Katie, an active three-year-old who was full of energy and had an adventurous spirit. She wanted to be very independent, including wanting to go her own way all the time and refused to travel in a pushchair. Her mum had a younger baby too and so Katie would often be confined to a double buggy when she took them out, so I tried to allow her to walk and have some degree of freedom on our own excursions to and from nursery. The problem was, Katie was a runner! She was one of those children who, before you even realised it, was running off down the street on her own. So I had to be very mindful of balancing her desire to be free with keeping her safe. She did not want to hold my hand and would often have a tantrum if I asked her to, so we came up with our own compromise. If Katie wanted to stay out of the pushchair, she had to hold onto it. Then once we got to the local park she was allowed to let go and run to her heart's content. I saw this an example of tough love, encouraging Katie to do something she didn't want to do (hold onto the pushchair) in order to keep her safe. The reward for her came in being allowed to walk and not strapped into a buggy and being able to run free once in the safe space of the park.

Emotion coaching

Reading this discussion of effective parenting styles reminded me of Gottman et al.'s work around emotion coaching. His research found that parents responded to their children in four distinct ways: disapproving, dismissing, laissez-faire, and emotion coaching. They found that often parents reacted to their children's behaviour without taking their emotions into account (Gottman, Katz and Hooven, 1996). In the cameo, you can see how different responses will either escalate the issue or help it to be resolved. An emotion coaching response is the best option to adopt because it validates feelings and accepts all emotions. A key belief that underpins this approach is that feelings themselves are always acceptable, but the way we act or react when feeling certain ways may not be acceptable. For example, although I feel cross with my friend, it is not OK to hit them. Feeling cross is sometimes understandable and, like all emotions, is an accepted way to feel, but we still need to monitor how we respond when we have this feeling.

Responding to children using different response styles

Context: A child has spent a long time drawing a picture and then, at snack time, a full cup of milk is spilled all over it.

Disapproving – Oh no – what did you think you were doing? I told you to move your picture before snack time.

Dismissing – Don't worry about it – it doesn't matter. We don't cry over spilt milk.

Laissez-faire – Sorry about that but I'm sure you'll manage to clean it up …

Emotion coaching – You must feel really upset, you spent a long time drawing your picture. Let's find some paper towels and mop it up and then when it's dry we can colour it in together.

An emotion coaching response recognises our natural ways of responding to stress and anxiety, when we get that hit of cortisol and are in freeze, fight or flight mode and offers a calming way out. This is because it is a non-judgemental stance and one in which the adult does not take sides or rely on the power dynamic to resolve the issue. It begins by empathising with the child and validating and accepting the emotions involved. With young children we tend to do this by labelling the emotions, saying something like, "You're feeling sad because mummy has gone to work. She will come back later. It's OK to feel sad – while you wait for mummy to come back shall we play together?" Once we have acknowledged the feelings, we can further explore the issue and set any boundaries or limits as appropriate.

Responding to children's emotions does not mean accepting all behaviours; sometimes we will need to explicitly explain why certain behaviours are not OK. Then we may need to problem solve with the child or children to resolve the issue together. Emotion coaching can also help children to 'own' any problems and enables them to become more independent in the future because it offers them strategies to use when the adult is not there. For example, when children are playing on their bikes and bump into each other, can they respond appropriately and calmly and continue playing? Chapter 8 explores using the problem-solving approach to conflict resolution in relation to helping restore relationships between children.

Using an emotion coaching approach, Widcombe Acorns

Our staff have completed emotion coaching training and we talk about feelings a lot, by acknowledging and validating feelings. We are empathetic and sympathetic and try to support children's friendships. For example, if a child falls over or comes in upset, we'll try to understand what's happened. We talk about feelings, about what feeling is, and how it would feel to feel like that. Emotion coaching for us is a cooperative approach to help them self-regulate their emotions so that they can deal with different situations. It also helps them to reflect upon what has happened and if they've not reacted in a way that's made the other person feel good about themselves, this approach helps them to know how to respond next time.

We teach the children that we all feel angry, we all feel jealous, or upset about things and that's fine, it's just how to deal with those feelings. We would say something like, "I can understand that you feel upset about this and that's fine, I would feel like that too. Let's see, what can we do about this, so that we're not getting really cross and hurting others, what do you think is the solution?" We try to get children to think of solutions and to regulate their emotions, with a bit of support. We are giving them the tools to rely on, hopefully, for the rest of their lives, so that once they move on from our setting, they can cope with those kind of feelings and not cause harm to others!

Do parents want us to love their children?

Whether parents want us to love their children will differ from family to family and child to child. As a parent myself who has used various different childcare settings over the years, I can say that from my own perspective I did want the educators to love my children. In fact I deliberately chose settings that I felt would be loving as well as being play-based and fairly small. However, I have spoken with friends who have expressed feeling slightly anxious that their children might love the educators more than them, so they are not too keen on professional carers loving their children too much, in case this happened.

Alison Shires, Snapdragons Nurseries

We share with parents that we are *in loco parentis* and want their children to feel safe and secure in our setting. However, we have noticed that some parents feel guilty about the number of hours they spend in the setting and a child then saying they love a member of staff can exacerbate issues! So we always consider how a parent would feel if a child says, "I love you" to a member of staff and we try to have open discussions with parents while maintaining professional boundaries.

It really helps as a whole staff team to have thought through what we mean when we talk about love in our settings so that we can share this with parents from the outset. Having a policy that covers this can be very beneficial and it is discussed in more detail in Chapter 3. Building a positive relationship with families is key to having a shared understanding of terms and preventing any potential difficulties that could arise. Consulting parents about what they want for their children in our care is often a good starting point. Chapter 8 thinks about how we can further develop our relationships with parents and carers.

Sally Kirby, Headington Quarry Foundation Stage School

I sometimes feel I am a replacement mum in school. I've had some parents who joke that their child loves me more than them, but I don't think any seriously think this is the case, they know it's a different relationship at school than at home. Parents want us to show love and care to their child and nurture them during their time with us. At school our relationship with their children is caring but we also have clear professional boundaries. Each individual key person gets to know the children and sets these boundaries. We also want to avoid children being too reliant or dependent on one particular person so we build relationships with all of the children. When children are established and settled, I would describe it as love between us and them. Often this is towards the end of the year, and then you have to say goodbye, which can be very difficult.

Page researched whether mothers want professionals to 'love' their children and the importance that they attribute to love as part of their decision-making processes (Page, 2011). She studied mothers going back to work when their baby is not yet one and love, with all its complexities, is problematised as an issue to be resolved. She concluded that all the parents in her study did indeed want the professionals to love their children, in terms of the way they interacted with them, but they did not always use the term 'love'. Due to the fact that some parents may feel uncomfortable in using this term, as educators we can explain to parents that we want to hold their children in mind and enjoy their company and whether or not the word love is used, we can certainly adopt a loving pedagogy.

Read builds upon this notion, describing the action of parents sharing the care of their precious children with professionals as an "act of faith" and one that educators should respond to sensitively and with "a commitment to loving engagement" (Read, 2014: 68). Parents are entrusting someone that they most treasure in all the world into our care, which is a real privilege. It stands to reason that we should therefore respond to these children lovingly and treasure them ourselves.

As educators we need to have an understanding of how love fits within our role and in an attempt to meet this need, Page developed an understanding of what she deems 'professional love' and set up the Professional Love in Early Years Settings (PLEYS) research project, which investigated, "the conceptions and practices of love, intimacy and care in early years settings" (Page, undated: 5). The findings of this study were used to develop a toolkit aimed at educators to be used as a professional development resource and to educate the general public about professional love. You can find out more about this project at https://pleysproject.wordpress.com/ and professional love is further discussed in Chapter 3.

Baby W's story, Pebbles Childcare

Going back to work with your baby in tow is always going to be with mixed feelings; particularly when in home-based childcare, it's very different to dropping your child into another room before heading to another part of the building for the day – in home-based childcare you don't have that option. And so it was important to me that this didn't impact on W's development in any way, which is why I feel so blessed that she is growing up in a home-based childcare provision as the 1:1 loving relationship with Bridgit that she has developed has definitely contributed to the confident, sociable child she is now. When you place your child into childcare in any form, you hope that the person looking after your child will love them and care for them in your absence. And the relationship W has with Bridgit is exactly that and it's so lovely to see how happy Bridgit makes W. And, as a parent, that's all you can hope for in a keyperson. It is evident the genuine love Bridgit has for W and, as a parent, I feel incredibly lucky that W is able to access this family-esque childcare during her earliest years.

So although occasionally educators are afraid to use the term 'love' in relation to their work with young children, this must not hinder our practice. A loving pedagogy is an appropriate approach to take when considering the education and care of very young children. I do, however, believe that we should call a spade a spade here and use the terminology of love, and face up to the additional challenges that using this language can bring.

Child protection and safeguarding concerns

The words 'love' and 'loving' can have sexual connotations in the English language and clearly, as educators, we should safeguard children as our highest priority. I have come across educators who are worried about cuddling children or are very conscious about the way they use touch during the course of their day, which is another challenge to overcome. However, there is lots of research that tells us that touch is vital to young children's wellbeing and physical touch is an important part of human relationships – and encourages the release of oxytocin, otherwise known as the love hormone. Physical contact is very important in helping us to develop secure attachments and feelings of trust and security. This is explored in more detail in Chapter 4.

Many educators feel that child protection can be a barrier to acting in a loving manner to children and offering them the emotional support they need (Campbell-Barr, Georgeson and Varga, 2015; Piper and Smith, 2003). Concerns over child protection have sometimes overridden natural methods of affection and care. For example, one foster carer was advised not to allow their foster child to join the family for breakfast in bed due to safeguarding concerns (Byrne, 2016). Such advice stems from fear of loving actions being misinterpreted in some way and therefore is a defensive strategy employed for the sake of self-preservation. However, it could be argued that these fears will lead to a dichotomy of care with some children supported in loving ways and others less so.

Some settings are over cautious when thinking about positive touch and have very strict guidelines on how educators can physically interact with children. I remember talking to one of my students who had worked for a large holiday club playscheme over the summer and she had been shocked at their policy for touch. She was taught that if a child runs over to hug you, you put your arms up in the air so that you under no circumstances hug them back. She felt that this was a very dismissive approach and one that ignored children's emotional needs. When she raised this with her managers, she was told that the policy was in place due to fear of litigation and they wanted to avoid any smears on their reputation. Chapter 4 explores the tactile nature of love and how educators can respond in more detail.

Educators' responses in relation to child protection and safeguarding concerns

I interviewed several educators prior to writing this book and asked them why they thought that the term 'love' was sometimes seen as taboo in an early childhood context, or if they would use the word love in their work. Here are a few edited responses:

> I think it's crazy that we don't! [use the word love] I don't know whether they're thinking of the sexual side of love because it's love. I don't know. But there's so many different types. Love is such a broad term and there's like a spectrum of love, isn't there?

> I think people feel that by referring to it as love you're somehow crossing a line that you shouldn't cross … and I think people are so careful to say the right thing and to do the right thing.

> But I think love, the word love, people assume it's inappropriate. But I don't think they're seeing it in the bigger picture. It's not the same love that you have for your children, it's not the same love that you have for your family and friends, it's a professional love. I think people are too afraid to say it because they think it's the wrong thing to say and everyone's trying to be so PC and to say the right thing and that we're here as educators and not as nurturers and I think that actually they have to go hand in hand in order for the children to progress. I think they need you to be there caring for them in place of a parent when they're here but also educating them alongside.

> I previously felt very uncomfortable with the idea of professional love because of the media and safeguarding stories I had heard. From talking to Tamsin, I now have more understanding about it and how to use it appropriately in the classroom. I am not afraid of showing professional love because young children need to see it and feel it from role models they are around. I have also found that it is ok to give 'appropriate reassuring hugs and cuddles' as they are an essential part of working with young children.

Is love enough?

Simm's raises an important point about the retention of early childhood educators, who sometimes stay in a job where they may feel undervalued because of their strength of feeling for the children in their setting, because they love them (2006). Anecdotally, I have also found that educators say things along the lines of: "Although I might get paid more on the checkout of a supermarket, I love the children too much to leave!" This raises the issue that the early childhood sector might be relying on emotional ties and human attachment to retain members of staff. If this is true, it will weaken the argument for better pay and conditions. If educators are staying because they want to, they feel the rewards of being with the children that they care for so deeply outweigh the disadvantages of low pay and poor benefits. It will be easy for these educators to be taken for granted and for them to remain undervalued.

Again, this is a problem relating to professional love. If our feelings did not come into it, we might not want to continue with the job on the levels of pay and conditions offered. However, many people tend to follow a career pathway that fits with their interests and things they find enjoyable, after all: "One loves that for which one labors, and one labors for that which one loves" (Fromm, 2013: 51). I have been overheard saying in the past that I really love my job and would do it without being paid – just don't tell my employer that! Therefore, it could be argued that having a loving peda-gogy might actually hinder the professional status of early childhood educators, because it could encourage them to be viewed as surrogate parents, rather than as professionals. This notion is further explored in Chapter 3. Attachment and building relationships is, however, a vitally important part of our role as educators and one that could never be detached, regardless of how helpful it could be to our cause!

Trauma and attachment-aware settings

There is now a wealth of research into the impact of adversity and the importance of building early relationships and attachments. We need to be aware of how trauma can impact our children and, in my view, developing a loving pedagogy as an approach can be part of the healing process for these children. Adverse childhood experiences (ACEs) are defined as, "Highly stressful events or situations that occur during childhood and/ or adolescence" (Brennan et al., 2019: 4). They can be one-off experiences or more prolonged and sustained threats. ACEs could be thought of as childhood adversity or trauma that babies, children or young people are exposed to and are more common than one might imagine. Research suggests that in the UK almost 50 per cent of adults experienced at least one form of adversity during their childhood or adoles-cence (Brennan et al., 2019). ACEs can include all types of abuse, parental separation, witnessing domestic violence, mental illness, alcohol or drug abuse, incarceration. The term ACEs was coined by the American Adverse Childhood Experiences Study (Felitti et al., 1998), which found a relationship between these experiences at a young age and multiple health risks later in life, including links to the leading causes of death in adults. In addition to the ACEs included by this study, it is generally accepted that other potentially traumatic experiences can also have a significant effect on children's wellbeing, for example experiencing a bereavement at a young age, bullying, poverty, being in care and facing discrimination or peer rejection.

Such experiences can lead to a child being subjected to toxic stress, which has a detrimental impact on wellbeing into adulthood. This can have long-term damaging effects and the impact can even be passed on to future generations. Toxic stress is when a person is unable to control their stress levels and continually has a high level of cortisol in their body. Cortisol is the main hormone naturally released when we feel stress or anxiety. That moment we go into freeze, fight or flight mode, when our brain recognises a state of emergency, the amygdala takes over and we cannot think rationally. You may have heard this referred to as the 'upstairs and downstairs brain' (Siegel and Bryson, 2012). When we are calm, we can think before we act and we are using the thinking part of our brain, the cerebrum, referred to as the 'upstairs brain'. When we are under threat, stressed or anxious, our 'downstairs brain' takes over which is responsible for our emotional state and our survival instinct. We are no longer calm, as our body pumps cortisol and adrenaline into our veins preparing us to run our fastest away from danger or be at our strongest to fight. We need to calm down and allow time for our upstairs brain to regain control.

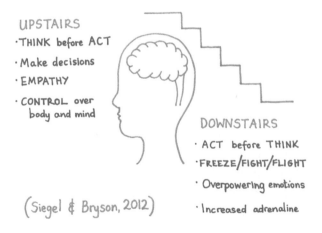

This response is designed as a survival technique to save us from threat or danger, so a low level of cortisol is OK. However, many children, and adults, live in this state of red alert all the time, leading to long-term physical and mental health problems. If a child is growing up with healthy attachments and adults who can help co-regulate their emotional states, they will, "Develop healthy stress response systems. Even children who experience serious hardship can still develop 'resilience' if they have the buffer of a strong, supportive attachment relationship" (Brooks, 2020: 23). Sadly, children who do not have these relationships in their lives may not develop these healthy response systems.

In conversation with Rebecca Brooks, towards a trauma and attachment-aware setting

Becoming a trauma and attachment-aware setting is not about a training course or a checklist. It is a process that will involve not only all members of staff, but also the setting's policies, procedures, values and systems. It will mean, for instance, a focus on the importance of relationships, understanding that healthy dependence must come before healthy independence, being curious about children's behaviours and reactions, acknowledging and empathising with emotions, co-regulating, responding to a child's developmental stage rather than their age, and cultivating supportive home-setting relationships. But what might this look like in practice?

Kara's setting responds to her severe separation anxiety by ensuring her key worker greets her every morning. The key worker, Kara and her carer enter through a side entrance to a quiet room away from the noise and bustle and together engage Kara in a familiar activity. When it is time for the carer to leave, she gives Kara a transition object – a soft scarf scented with the carer's perfume – to reassure her that she will be coming back for her. At home time, the key worker provides a transition object from the setting to reassure Kara that she will be returning soon.

At his previous setting, Khalid got a reputation as a difficult child. His key worker at his new setting is curious about his behaviour and makes notes on Khalid's outbursts, including what was happening before each one. Over time the key worker recognises that Khalid's outbursts are often linked to transitions between activities. She introduces a visual timer to help him manage transitions, and short sensory activities designed to help him regulate his internal state, such as a few bounces on the mini trampoline, or a crunchy snack.

Sofie is withdrawn and silent at her setting. She does not interact with other children or adults. Her parent reports that she is completely different at home and often has serious outbursts and meltdowns. Over a series of meetings, Sofie's parent and the setting staff explore the adverse circumstances of Sofie's early months and recognise that Sofie is exhibiting an avoidant attachment style at the setting. Staff work to increase Sofie's sense of safety by implementing structured routines supported by visual prompts, maximising her 1:1 time with her key worker, being curious about her emotional state and helping her to identify her feelings and needs, and supporting her to be appropriately dependent on adults.

Children who have experienced disrupted attachments and early life trauma can be impacted in their physical, cognitive, social and emotional development. However, the brains of young children are plastic and adaptable, and an attuned early years setting, working with the child's parents or carers, can make a huge difference in the life of a child.

Part of developing a loving pedagogy is being trauma and attachment aware and ensuring that our practice is informed by this neuroscience and approach. As Brooks has said, this is not something which we can adopt overnight and tick off on a list somewhere. It is part and parcel of our whole ethos. Here are some suggestions of where to start:

- Ensure all members of our staff team understand about ACEs, trauma and attachment through engaging in professional development.

- Include being trauma and attachment aware in our policies and procedures.

- Get to know our children and families and be aware of their backgrounds, whilst avoiding making assumptions about their upbringing or ACEs.

- Reframe 'attention-seeking' children as 'attachment-seeking' children.

- Use strategies like emotion coaching and problem solving.

- Offer times in our routine to check in with children.

- Prioritise wellbeing for staff and children.

- Provide calming areas, e.g., a den or pop-up tent filled with cushions and blankets.

- Use sensory resources and engage in sensory play, like bubble blowing.

- Have calming strategies up our sleeves and get to know which work well for specific children.

- Provide a visual timetable and Now/Next boards to help children understand the routine of the day.

- Role model having a calm attitude and demeanour.

- Use natural consequences for children when possible. For example, if a child has deliberately broken a toy, do not replace it immediately. Instead, let them play without it for a while. This helps them to develop an understanding of cause and effect.

- Avoid public praise or reward systems built on social compliance. Instead use labelled praise and encouragement.

David Wright, Paint Pots Nurseries

Recently, we have developed our approach to children's behaviour, based on trauma-informed care and the ACEs research. Our policy is now called 'Understanding and Supporting Children's Behaviour'. This is a definition of love for me. We are seeing beyond the behaviour to the distressed child. We are asking the question 'What has happened to you?' instead of, 'What's wrong with you?' For the adult, this can require emotional maturity and self-regulation in order to support these children, whose distressed behaviour can sometimes be very challenging. The love element in this relationship is to put the child's needs before our own.

In summary

Developing a loving pedagogy is not an easy approach to opt for or one that will always be plain sailing. In fact, it can lead us into some tricky and difficult waters. Parents may not want us to 'love' their children or may have additional concerns relating to child protection and safeguarding. In addition, loving our job and wanting to be with the children can even be damaging to our career pathways if it keeps us in a job where we are undervalued and underpaid. However, in my view, developing a loving pedagogy is the most nurturing approach that a setting can adopt. It can encompass strategies such as loving kindness, emotion coaching and incorporate trauma and attachment awareness. This means that children who attend a setting who have adopted this approach will not only feel loved, they will be loved and their needs will be kept central to the whole provision.

Fromm considers love and loving to be an art, one that we can learn and improve on over time (2013). He thinks about it in terms of learning the theory and living the practice. Perhaps this is a helpful way of solving the problem of love within early childhood. If we treat our loving pedagogy as an approach to be mastered and skills that can be honed and developed over time, we might find it becomes less of a problem to be dealt with and more of a way of life.

Questions for reflection

1. What can you say to reassure parents and carers who might not want you to 'love' their children?

2. When responding to children and their behaviour, to what extent do you validate their emotions and accept their feelings?

3. How can you master the art of loving the children in your care?

References

Brennan, R., Bush, M., Trickey, D., Levene, C. and Watson, J. (2019). *Adversity and Trauma-Informed Practice: A Short Guide for Professionals Working on the Frontline.* Young Minds. Retrieved from https://youngminds.org.uk/media/3091/adversity-and-trauma-informed-practice-guide-for-professionals.pdf.

Brooks, R. (2020). *The Trauma and Attachment Aware Classroom.* London: Jessica Kingsley Publishers.

Byrne, J. (2016). Love in social care: necessary pre-requisite or blurring of boundaries. *Scottish Journal of Residential Child Care, 15*(3), 152–158.

Campbell-Barr, V., Georgeson, J. and Varga, A. (2015). Developing professional early childhood educators in England and Hungary: where has all the love gone? *European Education, 47,* 311–330.

Felitti, V., Anda, R., Nordenberg, D., Williamson, D., Spitz, A., Edwards, V., Koss, M. and Marks, J. (1998). Relationship of childhood abuse and household dysfunction to many of the leading causes of death in adults: the adverse childhood experiences (ACE) study. *American Journal of Preventive Medicine, 14*(4).

Fromm, E. (2013). *The Art of Loving.* New York: Harper Perennial.

Gottman, J., Katz, L. and Hooven, C. (1996). Parental meta-emotion philosophy and the emotional life of families: Theoretical models and preliminary data, Journal of Family Psychology, 10(3), 243–268.

Lexmond, J. and Reeves, R. (2009). *Building Character Report.* UK: Demos. Retrieved from www.demos.co.uk/files/Building_Character_Web.pdf.

Page, J. (2011). Do mothers want professional carers to love their babies? *Journal of Early Childhood Research, 9*(3), 310–323.

Page, J. (undated). *Professional Love in Early Years Settings: A Report of the Summary of Findings.* Sheffield: University of Sheffield. Retrieved from https://pleysproject.wordpress.com/pleys/summary-of-findings/.

Piper, H. and Smith, H. (2003). 'Touch' in educational and child care settings: Dilemmas and responses. *British Educational Research Journal, 29*(6), 879–894.

Read, V. (2014). *Developing Attachment in Early Years Settings: Nurturing Secure Relationships from Birth to Five Years,* 2nd edn. Abingdon: Routledge.

Siegel, D. and Bryson, T. (2012). *The Whole-Brain Child: 12 Proven Strategies to Nurture Your Child's Developing Mind.* London: Robinson.

Simms, M. (2006). *Retention of Early Years Practitioners in Day Nurseries,* Paper presented at the British Educational Research Association New Researchers/Student Conference, University of Warwick, September 6, 2006. Retrieved from www.leeds.ac.uk/educol/documents/157460.htm.

3 Professional love

Introduction

I have found from visiting and talking with hundreds of educators in early years settings and schools that love really is all around, yet seldom talked about. Most professional educators would describe their relationships with the children as loving, however, Page (2014, 2017, 2018) cautions practitioners away from the idea that loving children in professional roles is somehow easy. Page's practice experience alongside her years of research into the place of love in professional caregiving roles have made her resolute about the fact that: "It takes a huge amount of resolve on the part of the caregiver to work sensitively with children and parents in a manner that is respectful, equitable and professionally appropriate" (Page, 2014: 127). This chapter explores these themes and the idea of professional carers and the use of the word 'love'. It also considers how we can include and embed love within our policy as well as enact love in practice.

A matter of terminology

With regard to a professional love, I know that many practitioners are concerned about using the word 'love' and how this might sound to others. Yet if you talk to these practitioners, they say something like, "Oh you do love them all…. but you would never use that word" (Elfer and Page, 2015: 1773). As Chapter 2 has discussed, this needs to be acknowledged but not hinder practice. It is perfectly acceptable and appropriate to adopt a loving pedagogy and embed professional love into our settings and practice.

David Wright, Paint Pots Nurseries

For me, it is about unconditional love. The problem with words is that they can be powerful cultural references, shaped and adapted over time to form the basis of attitudes and beliefs. Thus 'love' has become associated in the general consciousness with romance, sex, protection, maternal instincts, abuse, etc. This is problematic when applied to organisational care. We sometimes encounter concern from parents/carers that their 'love' for their child could be displaced by his/her affection for another adult. There may be concern about whether it is appropriate for a carer to provide love, particularly males – what sort of love? Does love involve touch, caress, cuddling, kissing? When is this appropriate or inappropriate? What is the crossover with safeguarding?

Robust organisational culture is key to the establishment of a common understanding of what constitutes professional love and the associated appropriate behaviours which is important because this forms the perception that parents and carers have of our settings.

Page is clear about what she means by professional love when she explains:

In using the term Professional Love, I want to indicate a quite particular discourse of which early years professionals should be expected to articulate; a set of practices which I would expect to see implemented in early years settings; and, thirdly, a culture of open, collaborative and reflexive enquiry in the early years setting.

(2018: 125)

This is not simply a handy phrase to use to describe love in a professional early years context. It is deeper than that and can be a powerful tool to frame our whole ethos.

Educators responses in relation to 'professional love'

I interviewed several educators prior to writing this book and asked them what they thought professional love meant. Here are a few edited responses:

I would often say I love that bit of my job or I love that child. I don't mean like I love my [own] children. I do mean professional love yes. So I would put those professional brackets round it. But I would still use those words and I would use them to the parents as well.

Professional love is more what we do. I don't think that I would ever have to worry about whether I force those feelings or not because it's about what this job is. It's about being loving, even when you don't feel like being loving. That's actually the most important part of this job, in a way, how a parent would be to a child and that's about behaving in a way that is loving. So yes, professionally, it's really important that that definition of what loving is put into practice. But I don't know if I've really thought about how to define in on a daily basis. It's fairly instinctual you know.

I think it's difficult because the word love covers such a vague concept and people have different meanings for it, there's lots of different types of love; how I feel about my family and how I feel about my friends … We definitely care for these children and we get along with them and we build up a really nice rapport with them over the year. But it's different, again. It is a different type of love. Like you were saying about professional love, I do feel it's different but I do feel there is love in a setting. We definitely care and want the best for these children and we do go out of our way as much as we can to make that happen really, to make them settled and happy.

We define 'professional love' as 'giving children what they need but not showing favouritism.'

Professional love

Professional love relates to the professionalising of an abstract concept. As discussed in Chapter 1, love could be discussed in terms of the intense feelings a parent has for a child, sexual desire or simply a very strong liking for something. Using the term 'professional' helps to define the parameters of the relationships involved and begins to address the complexities discussed relating to intimacy in settings. You might even think it sounds more formal and less intimate. Using the term 'professional love' perhaps separates it from 'parental love' or 'erotic love' and possibly gives permission for love to be redefined within the context of a specific setting.

In my view, using the term 'professional love' also provides educators with a language that they can use to accurately describe their relationships with the children in their care. It could also be argued that using this term gives permission to educators to 'love' the children in their care, as the vast majority of adults working with young children admit to having very strong feelings for them and having their best interests at heart. However, as discussed in Chapter 2, not all parents want educators to love their children in a professional setting (Page, 2011) and there are many complexities that arise once we enter into a discourse around this theme (Page, 2018).

In discussion with Chloe Webster, Pebbles Childcare

Having worked in day nurseries previously, both Bridgit and I are considerably mindful of affection, behaviours and remaining 'professional' and 'appropriate'. We have reflected upon whether this is more to do with how certain levels of affection or behaviours would be viewed by others in the setting or our own feelings regarding recent safeguarding breaches in the media. Looking back on relationships and our level of professionalism, perhaps we were subconsciously aware of 'professional love' and the need to remain 'professional'. But we wondered how easy it is to be equally affectionate and 'loving' towards a larger group of children that you generally care for within a bigger nursery or preschool environment?

Parents choose home-based childcare for their children as they want a 'home away from home' environment and so if we were to limit or restrict our affection/relationships with our children that would change the dynamics of the service we offer. Young children need loving and secure relationships to grow and learn from; and we pride ourselves on being an extension of these children's wider family community and adopting the family values that are so important for young children learning, love, empathy, compassion and understanding.

Many parents choose a setting based upon whether or not they deem it to be loving in nature. When I first considered childcare for my children, I thought carefully about which setting to choose. I had a sort of checklist in my head that went something like: Warmth? Loving interactions? Play? Outside area? Not too formal? And it was on this basis that my children began attending a lovely preschool near my home. I am sure I am not alone in this either. Having chatted with several parents and carers informally about why they choose a particular setting for their children, many of them said it was due to the friendliness of the staff, or the way they warmly interacted with their child when they went to look around. Very few said it was purely on cost or opening hours, although these aspects are important. Clearly this is anecdotal. However, research also suggests that many parents opt for the most loving approach when choosing childcare for their children. Therefore love is being sought within early childhood settings (Vincent and Ball, 2001).

Professional love must be viewed more as part of the role of a professional, rather than as a feeling or emotion to ensure that professionals are able to demonstrate this love, regardless of their feelings for the child. This is in line with Vincent and Ball's findings that parents would rather choose professionals who love and care for their children as opposed to those who are "only doing it for a job" (2001: 650). Being professional and efficient alone is not enough; warm and loving interactions are essential. However, a shared understanding of 'love', 'professional love' and 'professionalism' must be explored to demonstrate what a loving approach in early childhood would look like.

As professional educators, we usually try to do our jobs to the best of our ability. Our ethos and beliefs about our role underpin everything we do. Wood states his ideas about this as he outlines what we, as educators, do to enable our children to succeed in our schools and settings. He equates this to the parental role and says that talking about professional love is appropriate and valid because it demonstrates our commitment to our children in an ethical way (Wood, 2013). After all, we are acting *in loco parentis*.

Wood's claims about professional love as norms by which teachers operate

- We are committed to caring for and protecting our children.
- We will treat our children as individuals, with different needs and expectations.
- We will put their interests before our own.
- We will seek to teach them, "by precept and example", how to live and live well.
- We will encourage them to develop as thinkers, as learners, as members of a family, a circle of friends, a community and society.

- We will offer them our knowledge and understanding of language, culture and society but recognise that our knowledge is limited and insufficient and they will require also to learn from others.
- We will protect their health and safety and encourage the development of their physical strength and aptitudes.
- We will attempt to guide them towards accessing life's varied experiences at appropriate levels and stages.
- We will praise their successes, support them through their failures and encourage them to be aware that life will bring a share of both.
- Above all else, we will happily accept their short-term dependency and encourage, look forward to, and prepare them for, independence.

(Wood, 2013)

Professionalism

This discussion leads us to consider the notion of professionalism and how we can understand it in the context of loving relationships. Manning-Morton argues: "Professionalism in the early years must also be understood in terms of the day-to-day detail of educators' relationships with children, parents and colleagues; relationships that demand high levels of physical, emotional and personal knowledge and skill" (2006: 42).

Thus professionalism in an early childhood context must also include what educators do in practice and the relationships that they strive to build with the children. Elfer and Page (2015) conclude that there is little guidance, either in theoretical or practical terms, which supports educators to manage close relationships with children. This can, therefore, cause a problem if settings and schools fail to discuss in detail adult–child interaction.

Sadly, due to child protection concerns, a small minority of managers respond by stipulating strict guidelines or policies limiting touch and other adult–child interactions. This sort of response has led Byrne to describe, "a new form of abuse" that professionalism has created as he discusses the way that caregivers overlook children's "emotional needs for love and intimacy" (2016: 153). Byrne also asks the question, "Is there any place for 'love' in the professional helping relationship?" (2016: 153). He asks this in the context of Irish social care in residential child care. However, his points could be applied to childcare more generally. He concludes that, "Love and care are, and always will be, inextricably linked", and advises that to enhance as well as protect the relationships at the core of care work, child protection issues must complement rather than inhibit. Chapter 4 further considers this point.

Rebecca Brook's story: professional love as a foster carer

Many years ago, while I was waiting in the parents' room at the hospital, I saw a new dad holding his tiny baby. He was enraptured. His eyes were fixed on his baby's face to such an extent that he barely noticed my presence. It was a beautiful expression of the strength of love between a parent and a child. I was there as a foster carer to pick up another child – a newborn infant – and was struck with grief for a tiny child who was about to exchange the familiarity of her mum for the arms of a stranger. All children deserve to be raised by a person who feels and demonstrates this genuine warmth, affection and love towards them. Yet, when a child arrives in a foster carer's home, sometimes with very little notice, they are strangers, and the relationship has to begin from scratch.

I became a foster carer because I loved children. Yet I soon realised that there is a difference between a generalised love for children and developing an appropriate loving relationship that an individual child needs and deserves. When we care for other people's children, we do not replace their parents. We must carve a different kind of relationship, but the foundation must still be unconditional love and positive regard. If those feelings do not come naturally – and realistically they may not – we, as the adults, have the responsibility to pro-actively nurture that relationship.

When children arrived in my home, often with very little notice, the work of establishing that relationship would begin. There was no reason why the child would have any feelings of trust or warmth towards me, a stranger, and I had no expectations of that. Children would often be very frightened and unable to accept my comfort. So I would begin by prioritising the child's sense of safety through my tone of voice, through trying to provide comforting foods, smells, blankets and routines. I would pro-actively respond in loving ways as I waited for the love to grow. For young infants this might mean a lot of carrying and holding, looking into their faces, speaking and singing soothingly. For toddlers it might mean learning quickly to recognise and respond to their expressions of need, coming to their level, showing empathy, finding ways to soothe that did not make them feel overwhelmed or threatened. Over time, actions of love would translate into genuine feelings of love, with no expectation of reciprocation on the child's part.

People often say to me that they could not be a foster carer as they would get too attached to the children. Yet this is exactly what the children need. The experience of an attuned, attachment relationship will be foundational to the rest of their development. That may come at an emotional cost to the adult, but we can bear it for their sakes.

See further Brooks (2020).

This case study demonstrates how love and care are so 'inextricably linked' when Rebecca talks about her role as a foster carer. This could be described as the ultimate professional *in loco parentis* and must be incredibly difficult. It must also be very hard for children who find themselves joining another new family, wondering how long they might stay. Chapter 2 considers how trauma and attachment can have a huge impact on children and highlights how important it is for professional educators to have a strong loving pedagogy so that they can support these children as sensitively as possible.

Education settings are constantly hijacked by different agendas such as measuring progress, or safeguarding, which in turn is putting pressure on educators and further disadvantaging the children in their care. It could be argued that too great a focus on professionalism within early childhood education can actually diminish the role that love and care play within this sector (Rouse and Hadley, 2018). On the other hand, in my opinion, the early childhood sector lacks the recognition and status that it deserves, and so strengthening professionalism will also strengthen its professional demeanour from society's perspective.

Glorified babysitters or extension of mothers?

One of the reasons why early childhood settings can be undervalued is perhaps because the caring elements of the early childhood practitioner's role are often seen as an extension of the maternal role, rather than a professional (Vincent and Braun, 2011). This view diminishes the empowered image of women that feminist theory has fought hard to maintain, implying that early childhood educators are not professional carers, just as mothers are not professional carers. However, if we accept the *Oxford Lexico Dictionary* definition of a professional as someone who is "competent, skilful or assured" (2020), it could be argued that mothers and early childhood educators are indeed professional.

The PLEYS project, mentioned in Chapter 2, identified some confusion between educators who saw themselves in the role of mother and those who saw their role as distinct from parenting, although a huge overlap was acknowledged between love, intimacy and care (Page, undated). Other theorists have identified differences between 'natural' mothering and professional childcarers, both in terms of training and how they viewed themselves, revealing that successful childcare educators achieved, "a position more akin to professional detachment" (Saggers and Grant, 1999: 82). This could overlap with the PLEYS project, which discusses the ability of some educators to 'de-centre', when they can absorb themselves in responding to the needs of the child and remove their own needs from the equation. It could be argued that the ability to 'de-centre' is similar to detachment, which is counter to the idea that professional love manifests itself in an adult who is fully attached to the child. However, the ability to 'de-centre' could also be viewed as fully absorbing oneself in the child's needs, which is actually being less self-centred and more attuned, which is a very loving approach and not detached at all.

Alison Shires, Snapdragons Nurseries

Parents usually choose our settings because they need childcare. We always tell parents that they are the children's first educators and listen to their perspectives about how to care for their child. However, sometimes parents think we're only minding the children and forget that we're educators too – particularly with younger children. So we need to build up the relationship with the parents and give them examples of how the children are learning from our observations of the children.

Detached attachment

Vincent and Braun (2011) found when researching professionalism in the early childhood that the focus was on practice rather than theory and knowing content of policy in order to implement it. They argue that educators were more like technicians and less like professionals in status. Hopkins agreed, stating that, "The care of infants in day nurseries often becomes impersonal rather than intimate" (1988: 99). Drawing upon research from the 1980s, Hopkins explains that some nursery nurses still believed that a close attachment with an individual child could cause attachment issues with their mother and difficulties for staff when the child's main nurse was absent. They also found, in not forming intimate relationships with the children, the nurses were avoiding the pain for both them and the child when they had to part and the potential demands of children who always seek their attention. Menzies Lyth (1988) theorises that this type of impersonal practice could be a social defence system employed by the nurses to protect them from stress and emotional demands. This links with the idea mentioned earlier about professional detachment and Nelson (1990) refers to "detached attachment" when describing women who refrain from becoming too attached to the children they care for.

Saggers and Grant (1999: 77) found evidence to support this idea when they interviewed a childcarer who struggled with becoming too intimate with the children she cared for stating, "You learn to be a little bit more apart." Such ideas detract from the idea of a professional carer forming warm, close and loving relationships with the children in their care and add weight to the idea that professionals need to be detached. From my own experience, I do not think that this is still the case. In recent years there has been a wealth of data looking at things like how affection shapes a babies brain (Gerhardt, 2004) and the importance of attachment and positive relationships through the key person approach in settings (Elfer, 2006; Lindon, 2010).

Page has also demonstrated in her work around the adult's ability to de-centre that it does not have to be one or the other – either attached or detached. Through being able to de-centre, they still form a close relationship and experience intimacy on an emotional level with the child. This means that the ability to de-centre is not at all detached; it is, in fact, enabling the adult to purely focus on the needs of the child (Page, 2011, 2017, 2018).

In discussion with Lucy Waterman, the development coordinator for Love Early Years

Lucy was recalling a time when she regularly visited a setting on a consultancy basis. She remembers one little girl as being very quiet and, when she asked about her, the staff explained that she was very talkative at home but, for some reason, she didn't really talk at the setting. They said they just let her get on with it. After a few visits and playing alongside the little girl, Lucy was at a snack table and this little girl reached her hand towards Lucy. The girl's fingernails were brightly painted pink and Lucy commented on them and how beautiful they looked. This opened the door for communication as the little girl then started chatting about how her mummy had painted them. Lucy and the girl then chatted freely as the little girl talked about her rabbit and other things special to her. Over time, she became able to talk freely to other educators and children in the setting and this interaction changed her whole nursery experience for the better.

This moment that sparked a communication explosion would not have happened if Lucy had not sensitively responded in the moment. A simple comment from someone who has taken the time to be interested in a child's life can make the world of difference for some children. This personifies a loving pedagogy, when we notice things about children and we tune in to them, responding sensitively and giving them the message that we care about them. This is an example of an educator de-centering and focusing on the child's needs.

It is the reciprocal nature of love and how love fits within a relationship that also comes into play here. Coupled with the ethos of the setting, this becomes a very powerful force to enable children to feel welcome, valued, nurtured and loved.

Lisa Gibbons, Denmead Infant School: building relationships

My previous class were not going to let me build a relationship easily. They needed a determined, consistent and resilient approach. In short, I had to work for it! This is when I realised these children needed more than I had ever given before. They needed a strong, trusting relationship, which I later realised was 'professional love'. The relationship was firmly embedded and I loved each and every one of those children. I felt tied to these children and as they moved to year 1, it was challenging to let them go. They still shout out 'Mrs G' whenever they see me and I always get a flurry of hugs as we walk past each other in the corridor. Without knowing the term, I had established a loving pedagogy in my classroom. Something I now firmly believe in and will never look back.

Bringing love into policy

It is always useful to have a policy to underpin our ethos and pedagogy. Writing a policy also helps us to think in detail about what we do or do not do and why. So policies enable us to be clear and transparent about our practice. It gives us the opportunity to discuss this with our whole team, with parents, management committees or governors and also with the children. It enables us to consider important questions like, 'How do we demonstrate our love to the children in our care?' and 'What do we mean by a loving pedagogy?'

By involving the children in this discussion we can learn so much about what they think of and mean by the words love and loving. Which reminds me about a story that my friend told me when her young children, Imogen and Ben, were looking at a book about the body. Imogen said, "I know that all of those things are inside us, but really I am just made of love, lots of love!" and her brother Ben piped up, "And kisses, we have kisses in us too!" It was definitely a tearful mummy moment!

North Bradley Primary School: extract from vision statement

We strive to provide children with a happy, stimulating, loving, safe learning environment in which their intellectual, spiritual, personal, social and physical development can flourish. We believe that we should love and serve one another and make a difference in the world.

Our core values are:

- Love ourselves
- Love each other
- Love our world
- Love learning.

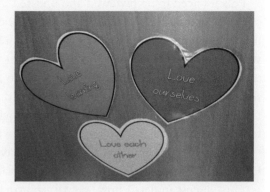

Peter Michell, the director of Mr Noah's Nursery School, lists the following advantages of establishing a professional love policy (undated: 12):

- Staff act in the context of clear thinking and of understanding.
- Parents understand the ethos and practice and are reassured that their young children will get the care and affection that they need.
- Children are not denied appropriate love out of our fear of getting it wrong. Rather their security and attachment are fostered.
- Explicit guidelines with examples help to ensure, not only consistency throughout the nursery, but relationships that are appropriate and supportive. There is less room for doubt and ambiguity.
- Defined boundaries facilitate freedom for staff within those parameters.

Marlis Jurging-Coles, St John's Preschool: professional love in policy

Grimmer's position on a loving pedagogy and her reasoning for making professional love part of settings' policies and curriculum inspired me to bring this topic up in a staff meeting. As a team we decided to consider implementing professional love in our policies. Initially, I met with our chairperson and brought forward the idea of a professional love policy. She agreed that it would be a good addition and said she would like to see the outcome of all our staff research. Any wording would have to be agreed before such a policy could be added. As a staff team we agreed that the greatest danger could be in the wording of a policy which could lead to misinterpretation and, in the wrong hands, even put children at risk of abuse. Therefore our policy and professional love must have clear set boundaries and be carefully worded to explain our position and approach in full.

Policies need to be reviewed and updated regularly to ensure that they still represent our current thinking and practice. It can also be helpful to include a section that outlines how we will respond specifically to the children, for example: 'When a child … adults will …' 'When a child wants to hold an adult's hand, the adult will reciprocate and hold the child's hand' or 'When a child climbs onto an adult's lap, the adult will allow them to sit side-on and loosely place an arm around them to prevent them falling off.' A policy can also be a useful way of broaching topics with new parents as we invite new families to read them in full and discuss any content with us.

Obviously there is no requirement to have a policy relating to professional love. However, I believe that having a policy in place is a great way of getting a whole staff team to discuss in detail how we will approach particular issues, like cuddles and children sitting on our lap. Ideally all policies are discussed as a whole team and written to reflect our practice and ethos, then shared with parents and children in an age-appropriate way. This is about deciding what we believe is right for young children and stating it for everyone to see.

Remember that every setting is unique and therefore we need to write the policy with our own context, circumstances and staffing in mind and it can be very powerful to also include the voice of the child when writing the policy. The introduction of this book touched upon how we can authentically listen to children in our settings. Once the team agree on the content of the policy, it is necessary to ensure that this is written up and shared with all stakeholders. Usually parents are asked to sign a copy of a policy to demonstrate that they have read and understood it.

A professional love policy could include the following points:

- How we have observed adults and children playing and interacting in our setting.

- A little theory about the importance of attachments and building strong, authentic relationships – what we believe and why.

- Our approach – how we will respond when a child wants a cuddle, or falls over, or says "I love you".

- An acknowledgement that there are different perspectives on this and a suggestion to read this policy in conjunction with the setting's safeguarding policy.

- How children have been involved or their voice is represented in the policy.

- How we will liaise with parents and carers.

- When we will review the policy and evaluate how things are working.

In conversation with Alison Shires, Inclusion Manager, Snapdragons Nurseries

Implementing 'professional love discussion in meeting and in practice'

"You're just like cuddling a marshmallow!" That's what a child said to me the other day, when I had popped into a room to observe. How wonderful; the child felt safe, secure, loved and able to freely share their feelings. But that doesn't just happen, particularly with this child who has been a challenge at times for all staff.

I have worked in the child care industry for over 37 years and during that time have seen a range of strategies, behaviour policies and the latest new fads, on how best to support children in our care. But the most powerful 'tool' we have to use with children is love. I believe that when children feel they are loved, valued, trusted and feel secure in our setting they will flourish. But, for some professionals this can be hard.

How do we show love, in a 'safe' way, in our practice? Could our best intentions be misinterpreted? This is why I feel it is important to visit 'love' in the setting and discuss what that means routinely in staff meetings, as well as role modelling it and being open and honest with parents. I know as a parent and grandparent I want my children and grandchildren to feel safe and secure. I would not have wanted to leave my most precious person in a 'loveless environment'. I know I could not have worked in an environment that did not allow me to show my love for the children. We now hear the term 'professional love' so perhaps this is an easier way for professionals to deal with the term 'love'?

How have we developed this in early years settings that I have worked in?

I have always started with having a policy. To begin, I write a range of statements and scenarios which I send to staff a week before, giving them time to discuss any issues that may arise beforehand. We do not always know how people will react and if parts of the discussion will trigger specific emotions. In the meeting we discuss these statements and the policy is written based on the discussions:

Is loving the children acceptable?

This statement normally brings out all the differing views around what is safe to do. This can lead to staff raising the question whether we can cuddle or kiss a child. I believe that as long as it's open and not hidden, that it's consensual, that it's not solely for our own satisfaction then that's ok.

Are male practitioners less likely to 'love' the child? How does being a man in this environment impact on practice? How does gender impact on daily practice? How could race and cultural diversity impact on love?

Some staff find these statements challenging to discuss. They may never have thought about it, However, if we want to feel safe and our children to feel safe in our settings we have to raise these issues.

How do we talk about love to the children? What do we tell them?

Valentine's Day can be a wonderful opportunity to celebrate love and what it means to the children. We have filmed the children's responses to the question, 'What is love?' and added it to their learning journey. Parents really enjoy looking at the comments. When asked why they love someone we had a vast amount of responses, ranging from, "They smell nice" and "They give the best cuddles" to, "They are my calm place."

With regard to touching children: how and when, what crosses the barriers?

Staff need to think about what would cause them to be concerned? Does the age of the child make a difference?

How do practitioners show love? Are we happy to accept cuddles, kissing or stroking? What is acceptable?

This can help staff to discuss when they feel they have seen practice that they are not comfortable with. As part of the senior leadership team, I have also found that if I have completed a staff observation before the meeting, focusing on touch, for example, completing a simple tally chart over a set time looking at cuddles and other physical contact, staff are often surprised to know how many times they engage with the children using touch.

We have found that by having the open discussion as a staff team, it helps to build a common understanding and all staff feel secure in their practice.

Reflective and reflexive practice

Being a reflective practitioner is one of the hallmarks of being an effective professional. When we desire to continually improve on our current practice and are able to think about what we do and how we do it, we tend to approach our setting with a critical eye. We strive to do what we feel is best for the children in our care. This links with our ability as an educator to de-centre as we focus more on the children and less on ourselves. Perhaps being critically reflective might require us to take a step back and therefore be a little more detached, although perhaps a better way to describe this would be to talk about being reflexive. This is when we not only reflect on a situation but we also self-reflect and think about how we may have had an impact on it.

Thinking about professional love and developing a loving pedagogy necessitates not only reflection on practice but also reflexivity on our part. So we need to take responsibility for our own thoughts, actions and feelings, think about the impact that they may have on the children and also respond sensitively in the moment to them. This allows us to be more effective in our reflection and also requires us to acknowledge any assumptions or preconceptions that we might have that would also impact on the children.

Aneesa Jangharia, Sunning Hill Primary School: letting children lead the play

Having worked in early childhood for a while, I have been in situations in the past where the end product was important, which means a lot of dictating from the adult. But through training and observing good practice in my recent work places, I'm more mindful of letting children lead their play and keeping certain activities open ended. For example, if the car/track printing turns into a huge swirling hand printing activity, it's absolutely fine! Not only have they discovered that colours can be changed but they've been able to explore and use their senses to their satisfaction. So much more learning has surely taken place. Allowing children to lead the play is being able to enjoy early years for what it really is and helps us to see the true meaning of pedagogy in early years.

Page (2018) suggests that thinking about professional love is a process that begins with an educator being 'self-aware' and available to think deeply about their own thoughts, actions and interactions. This will lead to the adult being able to 'de-centre' and concentrate fully on the child, rather than thinking about their own needs, which in turn will create 'emotional intimacy' and develop into a genuine 'reciprocal relationship' with the child. This is all in conjunction with getting to know the family really well and usually involves the parent or carer granting 'permission' for this relationship to develop, albeit without overtly saying this. It is often within this 'enduring mutual relationship' that professional love grows and develops (Page, 2018).

Occasionally, this relationship can develop in a much shorter space of time too. When I was teaching I unfortunately had to change schools partway through the school year. I only taught my reception class from September until Christmas and, in those days, the transition into school took about six weeks, so I had not taught all of the children for long. But I can honestly tell you that I built a strong and secure relationship with my class in that short term and I really loved them. I was sad to say goodbye and felt the pain of heartbreak!

In summary

I can accept that not everyone will want to develop or nurture a loving pedagogy, or want to discuss professional love. I do believe, however, that all children have the right to be loved in their lives and many early childhood educators will naturally love the children in their care, even if not all educators will feel this way. For some, as this chapter has discussed, these ideas may be overstepping the boundary of professionalism and it could be argued that loving the children in our care is a step too far. After all, the majority of the skills needed in order to become an early childhood educator can be learned and mastered regardless of our feelings for the children in our care.

However, it is my hope that because you have taken the time to read this book you are thinking about love. Children gravitate to those with whom they have strong connections and bonds and, generally speaking, they will respond and interact more with adults who take a full interest in their lives. It would be possible to do this without loving the children although, in my view, you would be missing out on the wonderful depth of relationship that a loving reciprocal relationship with a young child can give. Viewing professional love as a sort of process also describes how this arises fairly naturally as educators grow closer to the children in their care.

Some adults seem to have the 'X factor' when it comes to working with young children. Children automatically love them, they gel with boys and girls without really trying. Other adults are brilliant at making funny faces or using interesting voices when reading a story and the levels of engagement go through the roof! If we allow ourselves to build those close, secure relationships and show a genuine and authentic interest in the children's lives, we will develop the X factor for those children and they will probably gravitate towards us too. Dr Simms sums up the importance of this notion succinctly when she states, "Without professional love the sector is barren, with it our children will flourish for generations to come" (Simms, undated: 20).

Questions for reflection

1. How might you define 'professional love'?

2. What are your thoughts around love and intimacy and how do you relate these to parents and carers?

3. What sorts of statements would you include in a 'professional love policy'?

References

Brooks, R. (2020). *The Trauma and Attachment Aware Classroom*. London: Jessica Kingsley Publishers.

Byrne, J. (2016). Love in social care: necessary pre-requisite or blurring of boundaries. *Scottish Journal of Residential Child Care, 15*(3), 152–158.

Elfer, P. (2006). Exploring children's expressions of attachment in nursery. *European Early Childhood Education Research Journal, 14*(2), 81–95.

Elfer, P. and Page, J. (2015). Pedagogy with babies: perspectives of eight nursery managers. *Early Child Development and Care*, 185, 11–12.

Gerhardt, S. (2004). *Why Love Matters: How Affection Shapes a Baby's Brain*. Hove: Brunner-Routledge.

Hopkins, J. (1988). Facilitating the development of intimacy between nurses and infants in day nurseries. *Early Child Development and Care, 33*(1–4), 99–111.

Lindon, J. (2010). *The Key Person Approach: Positive Relationships in the Early Years,* London: Practical Pre-school Books.

Manning-Morton, J. (2006). The personal is professional: professionalism and the birth to threes practitioner. *Contemporary Issues in Early Childhood, 7*(1), 42–52.

Menzies Lyth, I. (1988). *Containing Anxiety in Institutions; Selected Essays: Vol 1*. London: Free Association Books.

Michell, P. (undated). A professional love policy. *Early Days Magazine, Professional Love edition,* Love Early Years.

Nelson, M. (1990). Mothering of others' children: the experiences of family day-care providers. *Signs, 15*, 586–605.

Oxford Lexico Dictionary (2020). Definition of 'Professional'. Retrieved from /www.lexico.com/definition/professional.

Page, J. (2011). Do Mothers want professional carers to love their babies? *Journal of Early Childhood Research, 9*(3), 310–323.

Page, J. (2014). Developing 'professional love' in early childhood settings. In L. Harrison and J. Sumsion (eds.), *Lived Spaces of Infant–Toddler Education and Care – Exploring Diverse Perspectives on Theory, Research, Practice and Policy*. Vol 11. International Perspectives on Early Childhood Education and Development Series. London: Springer Publishing (pp. 119–130).

Page, J. (2017). Re-framing infant toddler pedagogy through a lens of professional love: exploring narratives of professional practice in early childhood settings in England. *Contemporary Issues in Early Childhood, 18*(4), 387–399.

Page, J. (2018). Characterising the principles of professional love in early childhood care and education. *International Journal of Early Years Education, 26*(2), 125–141.

Page, J. (undated). *Professional Love in Early Years Settings: A Report of the Summary of Findings.* Sheffield: University of Sheffield. Retrieved from https://pleysproject.wordpress.com/pleys/summary-of-findings/.

Rouse, E. and Hadley, F. (2018). Where did love and care get lost? Educators and parents' perceptions of early childhood practice. *International Journal of Early Years Education, 26*(2), 159–172.

Saggers, S. and Grant, J. (1999). I love children, and four-pence a week is four-pence! Contradictions of caring in family day care. *Journal of Family Studies, 5*(1), 69–83.

Simms, M. (undated). Wings to fly: the validity and necessity of professional love *Early Days Magazine, Professional Love edition,* Love Early Years.

Vincent, C. and Ball, S. (2001). A market in love? Choosing pre-school childcare. *British Educational Research Journal, 27*(5), 633–651.

Vincent, C. and Braun, A. (2011). "I think a lot of it is common sense. ..." Early years students, professionalism and the development of a "vocational habitus". *Journal of Education Policy, 26*(6), 771–785.

Wood, A. (2013). Is professional 'love' appropriate? *SecEd blog,* 12 September. Retrieved from www.sec-ed.co.uk/blog/is-professional-love-appropriate/.

4 Tactile nature of a loving pedagogy

Introduction

Often the first thing that educators think of and refer to when reflecting upon the notion of professional love is the hands-on nature of caring for young children. Babies and toddlers need warm, loving interactions and intimate care and many children will want to hold our hands or cuddle up for a story. We can clearly see the tactile nature of a loving pedagogy in these interactions and a stand-offish approach can feel too formal or even old fashioned!

However, cuddling or snuggling up with children as part of our professional jobs may feel for some people over and above our job description. Where do we draw the line? How can we protect ourselves from being vulnerable to allegations about our conduct while safeguarding children and balance that with providing them the emotional support and physical connection they need? This chapter considers some of these issues and suggests that we need to embrace (no pun intended!) the tactile nature of a loving pedagogy.

Types of touch

Touch is inevitable in our settings to a certain extent. Young children need us to hold their hand to guide them and keep them safe as they walk along the pavement and we might have to lift a child into their cot for an afternoon nap. When caring for younger children or babies, we will need to change nappies, clean them up after eating, messy play or even bathe them and put them to bed. All of these parts of the routine necessitate a limited amount of physical touch, but it is touching children beyond the necessary that can cause us anxiety in our settings. However, touch is vitally important to all of us, as this chapter will explain.

For the purposes of their research into haptic communication, that is using touch to interact with young children, Bergnehr and Cekaite (2018) identified five different functions of touch: controlling, affectionate, affectionate-controlling, assisting and educative. Controlling touch is when we try to direct the child or discipline them through touch and may involve holding, steering, lifting or other ways to direct the child's body. Affectionate touch is when we comfort, express praise, approval or fondness, for example through embracing, hugging or when a child sits on our lap. Affectionate-controlling touch is a combination of the first two, for example by stroking a child's arm or gently lifting a child with the purpose of controlling them. Assisting touch is when we help the child, for example helping to dress them, change their nappy or assist them at mealtimes. Educative touch is when we are guiding the child and using touch in educational situations, for example through tapping the child's fingers when counting, or gently touching the child's arm when referring to the concept of left or right (Bergnehr and Cekaite, 2018).

The majority of touch in our lives is not centred on sexual intimacy. However, many educators still feel uncomfortable or uneasy when thinking about physical interactions with children. In our daily lives we might use touch in a number of ways, for example support (hold hand, arm around), reassurance (squeeze shoulder, hold hand, arm around other), affection (cuddle, hug, sit on knee), security (hide behind, arm around), appreciation (high five), greetings (hello/goodbye, kiss, hug, handshake), rough and tumble (tickle, tag) etc. Many of these types of touch happen as part of our normal routine with young children, yet some are perhaps more accepted than others and settings need to make an informed decision and set their own specific boundaries after weighing up the evidence around the importance of positive touch.

The importance of touch

Research has shown how vital touch is for our wellbeing and being gently touched and lovingly held creates a positive chemical reaction in our bodies as opioids and oxytocin are released when we are touched in a loving way. As Mainstone-Cotton (2017: 19) points out: "These chemicals contribute to us having a good wellbeing, feeling good about ourselves and feeling loved."

Oxytocin is sometimes referred to as the 'love' hormone because it is produced when we hug, cuddle or feel safe and connected with another person. It is also produced when we stroke a pet or when we hear the voice or see the smiling face of someone we have a close bond with. Physically touching someone else is the best way to increase our levels of oxytocin and, at the same time, reduce our levels of cortisol, the stress hormone. You might remember from Chapter 2, although a little cortisol is helpful, too much cortisol can be damaging to our health and wellbeing. So let us aim to increase oxytocin and reduce cortisol!

While researching for this chapter I came across some interesting work by Professor McGlone and colleagues from Liverpool John Moores University, who explains that nurturing touch has a significant impact on the developing brain and we have special systems and nerves in the skin that love to be stroked. His research shows that there are two types of touch systems: discriminative, which is our first response to touch when we immediately feel the sensation, and affective, which is more about the emotional connection or the pleasant soothing feeling that the touch gives us and this has a very slightly delayed response (McGlone, Wessberg and Olausson, 2014). In a news article, McGlone explains:

> There's a release of oxytocin, a hormone that plays a fundamental role in our social behaviour. It has an effect on our dopamine levels, which is the brain's reward system; it impacts on the release of serotonin, which is connected to our happiness and wellbeing; it has an impact on our stress system; and it helps lower our heart rate.
>
> (Coffey, 2020)

His research has also found the optimum rhythm for stroking, which our bodies respond most pleasurably to, which he equates to that of a mother stroking and soothing her baby.

Additional research into this area discusses how slow, soothing touch has an impact on social bonding and can reduce feelings of social exclusion (von Mohr, Kirsch and Fotopoulou, 2017). This is because physical touch is one of the ways we express our emotions and interact with others on a social level. For example, if we feel angry – we might want to hit, disgust – we could push something away and sympathy – we may place our arm around someone (von Mohr, Kirsch and Fotopoulou, 2017). A wealth of research has also shown that stroking a pet can reduce anxiety, blood pressure and have a calming effect for both the pet and the human, and yet more research considers the benefits of physical contact and touch to combat loneliness and reduce stress levels and feelings of anxiety (von Mohr, Kirsch and Fotopoulou, 2017; Okruszek et al., 2020).

One study specifically looked at new-born infants and how they responded to gentle touch. Through gently stroking the skin on the babies' legs and using MRI scans to record the resulting functionality of the brain, the researchers were able to conclude that social and affective touch are both important when considering the development of sensory processing and our early brains (Tuulari et al., 2019). Research studies such as this confirm what educators of young children already know through practice. Tactile experiences are important and we can soothe or calm a child through a gentle touch.

Ollie and Nathan's story, Westview Day Nursery

Although they are only a few months apart in age, Ollie and his cousin Nathan both attend our setting but are based in different groups. One day Ollie was feeling sad and so Nathan came downstairs to comfort him. The series of photographs captures this beautiful moment.

Many educators plan interventions or include specific activities as part of their provision that rely on touch, such as dance or baby-massage. We can role model soothing and comforting others using touch, for example actively encourage children to hold each other's hands or put their arm around a friend who might feel sad or unsure. The case study from Westview is a beautiful example of how children can comfort each other and the case study from Kingscliffe shares how they have used dance and physical connection as a way of non-verbal communication with very young babies.

Liz Clark, Kingscliffe Day Nursery: developing a loving pedagogy through creative dance

The children from the babyroom at Kingscliffe Nursery dance every week with their practitioners. They initially worked with dance artist Liz Clark, developing their understanding of quality interactions though dance using two processes. The first was a very physical form of play, where children are lifted, rocked and swung by the practitioners, who always seek permission and read the cues from the children as to how those physical explorations should develop. Practitioners also engaged in a process they called 'mirror play' – tuning into children's spontaneous expressions in movement and reflecting these back by respectfully copying. The children were eager to engage in these movement conversations and, through these exchanges, the practitioners found that, because movements were amplified and altered over time, the dances developed in complexity and sophistication. They danced to music, but with virtually no talking, which enabled both adults and children to value what they do, and know, through their bodies. The impact in the baby room was profound as intimacy developed in those dances and co-regulation occurred between those taking part. The children chose to interact through touch and their other senses, becoming very immersed in the interaction. Dances were very often joyful and flowed in a way that was akin to a form of mindfulness practice, which was very beneficial for everyone's wellbeing. Babies were also able to lead the way in the sessions and show their creativity and ingenuity.

Our children and team use movement and dance as a tool for connection and communication with the children, which in turn, leads to an increase in wellbeing and involvement. This has a marvellous impact on levels of engagement, the children's sense of agency as well as their attachment. We've been able to celebrate their uniqueness and creativity all with a huge injection of fun!

(Sarah Yorkstone, Early Years Teacher, Kingscliffe Day Nursery)

To read more about this lovely collaboration visit: www.ourcreative adventure.com/dancingbabies.

In loco parentis

Many educators believe they should act as if they were the child's parent, which includes being physically affectionate towards the children. When I was conducting my own research one educator stated: "We hug children and sit them on our knee, in the same way that we would our own children." Another said: "If they need a hug, we'll give them a hug, it's those sorts of things that they might ask their parent for, if they're not there, we'll do our best to step in and support whichever need they have." And a third stated: "They need you to be there caring for them in place of a parent."

Loving touch, Pebbles Childcare

Cuddles and close physical contact are an everyday, normal occurrence in our setting, regardless of the child's age – our children are all incredibly tactile and we reciprocate this as and when they need/want affection. It is not only when children are sad or requiring emotional support – sometimes they just want to cuddle or sit on your lap and we are more than happy to reciprocate that – we pride ourselves on a family ethos and the children grow up in our care knowing that they will have their affection and physical contact reciprocated and this then cascades into their friendships and relationships with each other. Similarly, our youngest children require that physical closeness from the outset and being able to be fully present and physically close to them during settling in periods, feeding and care routines, enables us to forge the strong bonds we have developed with our children over the years and allowed us to successfully instil family values throughout our practice and pedagogy.

Children might miss out on the reassurance that they so desperately need because some adults are unsure of how to physically respond. This may be linked to the confidence or experience level of the particular educator. I have become more touch confident through being a parent myself, perhaps because I became more experienced at using physical touch as an interaction. Maybe it was the many nights spent gently stroking my child's cheek or rubbing their back to help to soothe them. I wonder if, when at work, I subconsciously think: 'How would I want an educator to respond to my child?' Having said this, being a parent is not a prerequisite for having a loving pedagogy and I would not want to imply this.

Lisa Gibbons, Denmead Infant School: an educator and parent's perspective

In addition to being a teacher, I have three children of my own and this also made me realise how necessary it is that they feel loved at school. My little girl, Poppy, was helped tremendously in her first year at school by her LSA [learning support assistant], who gave her the cuddles and attention she needed to feel safe and secure in school. Poppy would have many a wobbly morning, but a genuine smile and welcoming arms from Mrs J would get her into school. As an emotional girl Poppy needed the deep understanding and love from the adults in her class. This benefited her wellbeing and made all the difference to her at school. As a parent I was both relieved and felt so fortunate that Poppy had someone who really cared about her and was happy to give her a cuddle when she needed it. It made me think about the children in my class and how

I could engage more with their parents and think deeper about knowing the child as part of a family. In order to build connections and the relationship with both parents and children further, I started having additional conversations with parents, just little chats and comments so they knew that I really knew their child really well. The children could see us all as a unit and this helped build trust and security.

Alienating touch

As Chapter 5 explains, everyone likes to give and receive love in different ways and not everyone likes to touch or be touched. It is the same for children. Therefore, we must not assume all children will want to hold our hand, have a cuddle or be tickled. In fact for some children, being too hands-on might inhibit them and create a chasm between us and them. We need to be aware that for a small minority of children touch might be linked with abuse, neglect or painful memories and we need to remain sensitive to how our touch will be interpreted.

In addition, a few children may have sensory issues meaning that they perceive and feel touch in a slightly different way to others. This can be particularly true for children on the autistic spectrum. One of my own children, who has a diagnosis of ASD, does not always like to be touched. In fact, she is ultra-sensitive to it. For example, I might brush past her and she will shout at me, "Mummy, why did you push me?" The touch may have been so light that I may not even realise that I have touched her! So although this chapter focuses on using touch in a positive way with young children, bear in mind that there may be groups of children for whom it is not so positive.

Gloria's story

When Gloria was aged between two and five, she tried to communicate with others through touch. However, she did not always do this appropriately. She sometimes pinched children or poked children that she liked and wanted to play with because she did not know how to initiate social interaction. Her parent explained that she would have to literally follow Gloria around in toddler groups and her key person in her preschool had to do the same, because they were never sure when she would hurt another child. She usually did it with a smile on her face, which always seemed to make matters worse, and she became very upset when she was not allowed to play with the child she had hurt. By the time Gloria was attending primary school, the hurting behaviours

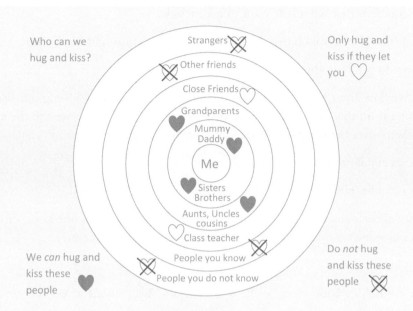

had stopped, but she began to kiss other children indiscriminately or while sitting on the carpet poke those around her or play with their hair or shoes. The teacher and Gloria's parents worked together and explained to Gloria that it was not always OK to kiss and touch other people without their permission. They used the above chart to help her to understand who it was appropriate to kiss and touch and who is was not.

What constitutes appropriate touch?

There are different reasons for using touch within our settings and it is important that we consider what constitutes appropriate touch when working with young children. It is a really good idea for all educators to talk openly about touch and then decide what appropriate and positive touch looks like.

So a good place to start is to invite a colleague to observe our practice and note down every physical interaction or positive touch undertaken within a set period of time. Through doing this we often realise we are using touch a lot more than we thought. After reflecting on practice, we need to decide what we believe is right for young children in relation to touch. Then, if we are part of a team, we should have a discussion about what constitutes appropriate touch in our whole setting. All educators need to share their views on this and differences must be respected. Drawing the line and setting the boundaries can be a very individual thing and it is important that all educators feel comfortable with any decisions made.

Key questions that we might want to ask include:

- Do we feel able to touch the children? How and when might we do this?

- Where do we draw the line?

- Can we 'kiss' their hurts better by actually kissing them, or by kissing our hand and rubbing it on the child or by doing an air kiss – "mwah" or do we ask the child to kiss themselves better or do we avoid kissing and kisses altogether?

- Can we cuddle a child – when might we do this?

- Can a cuddle/physical touch be initiated by us or just by the child?

- Do we allow a child to sit on our lap? How? Can a child sit on one knee, or on two knees or sideways on the lap? Can a child straddle me and face me?

- What about tickling?

- Can we hold a baby close – cheek to cheek? What about a toddler, or a three year old?

- Can we rub noses with them?

- Can we hold a child's hand?

- Can we 'high five' a child?

- Can we blow a raspberry on their tummy when changing their nappy?

These sorts of questions are very specific and encourage us to delve deeply into the precise types of touch that will or will not be allowed. It is really important that we look into this level of detail because this will provide clarity and avoid misunderstandings. The next step is to ensure that our policy reflects our approach and the more detail we can include in the policy the better.

A list of ways that we can appropriately touch our children could include:

Hug / Cuddle / snuggle
up / cwtch
High five
Fist bump, elbow bump!
Nudge
Shoulder squeeze
Pat arm / leg / shoulder
Lift child under the arms
Dance with them

Stroke (arm / back/ cheek / hair)
Rub back / tummy
Tickle
Rough and tumble
Swing child holding under their arm-pits or waist*
Hold child on our hip
Sit really close together
Hand on back
Blow raspberries on tummy
Thumb-war …
Sit on lap
Hold hands
Rub noses
Beep nose
Caress head
Hand shake
Kiss
Squeeze
Touch hand, arm, shoulder

(* *Never* swing a child holding their arms, it can damage their growing ligaments and joints)

As I was writing this chapter, an English report was published in response to Covid-19 and concluded that we need touch as part of a nurturing emotional environment in order to have positive wellbeing: "Basic human contact is just as central to a child's development as nutrition. Emergent neuroscientific evidence shows that nurturing touch is essential to foster the physical and emotional security that every child needs in order to thrive" (APPG, 2020: 6).

In conversation with Paula Lochrie, member of the APPG on the importance of touch

The All-Party Parliamentary Group on a Fit and Healthy Childhood *Wellbeing and Nurture: Physical and Emotional Security in Childhood* report was sponsored by John Moores University. The report was commissioned before Covid-19; however, enforced isolation that children have experienced as a direct consequence of the pandemic has made it more relevant.

The experience of nurturing touch for infants is now known to be an essential requirement for social brain development and the subsequent development of secure attachment. The report shows that during a child's transition into early years provision, the critical role of touch expands beyond the family environment to include early years practitioners and peers. The positive, contingent touch from early years practitioners has been demonstrated to increase on-task behaviour and reduce disruptive behaviour in young children.

It is important that classroom culture of pupil-to-pupil relationships are strong and attachment is high. Peer massage has shown that children become calm and support their peers, interpret kindness in a wide context, show empathy and consideration while practising positive social behaviours. This helps to build happy, relaxed and safe classrooms where children can trust one another.

Touch not only impacts on the short-term development of infants; it also has long-term effects, which contributes to lifelong learning. Positive touch from birth enables a child to bond with their carer, babies to learn about the new world around them, and is essential to communicate their needs further in life.

Recommendations from the report include:

- Emotional Health and Wellbeing is incorporated into Initial Training and Continued Professional Development for all health and education professionals involved in care and advice to children and their parents/carers.
- There is an immediate strategy to combat the adverse impact on the mental health of children and young people of social isolation beyond the pandemic. Services offering face-to-face contact and related activities should be commissioned especially in rural and other isolated communities.
- Positive touch work to become an established part of the school curriculum; possibly as a component of PSHE.
- All therapeutic practitioners (and those who work therapeutically with children in other contexts) to be registered by a government-approved professional standards accredited register.
- Department for Education through Ofsted to compile and cascade a compendium of best practice models and evaluations of affective touch strategies for classroom use.

- ■ Remodelling of training systems for officials and carers working with children in care to better educate them in appropriate touch and thus improve their practice.
- ■ The four Children's Commissioners to be involved in drawing up a set of agreed UK indicators for emotional health and wellbeing to be incorporated into all statutory children's developmental health assessment programmes.
- ■ Ensure that Sure Start Centres are integral to a new social isolation reduction strategy because they have the capacity to offer early intervention in a variety of locations (not exclusively more built-up areas).

For further recommendations from the report visit https://fhcappg.org.uk/wp-content/uploads/2020/07/ReportWellbeingandNurtureFinal140720.pdf.

We also need to take into account the needs and wishes of the child in relation to touch by closely observing children and noticing their body language, for example if a toddler holds up their arms to be picked up we can listen to the child's body language and act in the moment by picking them up. A helpful way to respond is to always talk to young children and explain why we are touching them and offer them the opportunity to reciprocate or express their wishes if they do not want to be touched. I have observed educators who forget to do this and approach a child from behind with a tissue in hand, and wipe the child's nose and then wonder why the child bursts into tears! It would be better to offer a tissue to the child and ask if they need help to blow their nose, or if they are unable to do this, explain, "I need to wipe your nose now to make it clean – there you are, all done!"

We also need to think about who the touch is for – who is it benefiting, us or the children? If we are feeling a bit low and think we need a cuddle and so we cuddle a child to help us feel better, that is not necessarily in the best interests of the child. But if they instigate a hug then that is different. Young children need to feel close to the adults who care for them and positive touch is part of that story.

Siena and Freddie's story, Widcombe Acorns

The children are sat on the carpet for singing time. Heidi, the adult, sits on a rug on the floor and three-year-old Siena sits in her lap. Heidi's right arm protectively holds Siena in place, while Heidi gently rests her left arm around four-year-old Freddie, who snuggles up into Heidi's left side. All three are looking happily at Diane, the preschool leader, and singing along with the 'Aiken Drum' song, comfortable in each other's company.

This was a very typical scene that I regularly observed as part of my research for my Master's dissertation. There was an air of warmth and affection as Siena happily sat on Heidi's lap and Freddie snuggled into her side. Heidi has also told me that she feels, "comfortable enough to cuddle them." Children being physically close to educators represents the tactile nature of a loving pedagogy and this observation could have been made in any number of settings around the world.

Bergnehr and Cekaite (2018) would describe this as an example of 'affectionate touch' used to show fondness and demonstrate approval. From their research, which considered touch in a preschool environment, affectionate touch was the most loving way that they observed touch between educators and the children in their care. This is also an example of children wanting to remain in close proximity to an adult they have an attachment with. Usually children only want to cuddle adults that they are familiar with and want to be close to.

Safeguarding issues

Safeguarding should always be our highest priority in our settings. As discussed in Chapter 3, discussion around child protection issues should complement our practice and not inhibit it (Byrne, 2016). Many educators are afraid to act in a way that they want to or find comes naturally in relation to touch because of fear that their actions may be misinterpreted or their intentions misconstrued (Aslanian, 2018; Piper & Smith, 2003).

Discussing the culture of fear and suspicion, Piper and Smith (2003) describe the 'moral panic' that has evolved around issues relating to touch in early childhood settings, with some settings and schools implementing 'no touch' policies. The whole idea of such a policy really upsets me, as I have read widely about how touch is vitally important for healthy emotional development and wellbeing. I also find it hard to imagine what would happen if one of those children were to fall and hurt themselves, or if another needed a cuddle in order to feel safe and secure. In my view, these settings are doing children a disservice as children are denied love, which we have established is a fundamental need.

In fact, in the light of the wealth of research that explains how vital touch is I would go further and suggest that a 'no touch' policy is neglectful and could fall into the realm of emotional abuse. I would recommend that educators continue to read around this area because understanding the importance of touch can enable us to gain confidence and reassure us that our approach is based on research and neuroscience and is the most appropriate ethos to adopt.

Despite this evidence, I regularly hear from educators who do not feel confident in physically interacting with the children in their care. Many students and inexperienced educators might be reticent about appropriate or inappropriate touch and adults of all confidence levels will naturally fear any repercussions if their caring touch is misunderstood.

In conversation with trainee teachers about touch when working with children

Joshua Bolton

As a male teacher, I am not affronted to being hugged by a child, but I would not feel comfortable and wouldn't initiate a hug. It's definitely something that I wouldn't decline, particularly in front of other adults. But I would be extremely conscious if there were no other adults in the vicinity.

Charlotte Proctor

For me, professional love was an area that I was always wary about. I was concerned with expressing emotions and affections because of the safeguarding boundaries. I have learned the importance of professional love and ways that we can implement it in our practice, safely and appropriately. Appropriate reassuring hugs and cuddles are an essential part of working with young children. It is important to consider your own and colleagues' understanding of this, particularly in relation to safeguarding and promoting children's welfare.

Francesco Mauro

I believe that men will always be perceived as being 'out of place' within the early years setting, and that is because in society nowadays men are told not to be caring … due to an unhealthy perception of what being 'manly' is supposed to be about. As a man and educator it is my duty to demonstrate to worried parents that everything is okay, because, if I'm comfortable with the children and the children are comfortable with me, there is nothing to worry about.

Reuben Burlingham

When I first went into school as a teacher, I was incredibly cautious and uncomfortable with what I was supposed to do as a man. Some of the children had sensory needs and needed touch from adults to be able to focus and participate. I found it difficult to show physical affection to even these children, despite it being something they required. However, throughout my practice so far, I have found it increasingly necessary to be a loving figure towards the children, especially in my school, where a lot of the children came from single parent homes. These children began to look to me as a father figure. They needed to know they were loved and I wanted to show them that a man can be a nurturing figure. Knowing there are young boys out there now who 'want to grow up to be like me and be a teacher', because of me, I'll take that as a huge reason to be a nurturing male and make sure the children know they are loved in the classroom.

Summer Redford

Even as a female teacher I am very aware of physical contact and would adjust myself to actively avoid unnecessary contact. When the children do initiate a hug my first instinct is to look to check there is another adult in the room. Whilst on my teaching practice, I have had experiences with a male TA [teaching assistant] who has asked me to walk a female child to the bathroom because he didn't feel comfortable even though it was my first day on placement and he was already working within the school.

In recent years there has been a drive to recruit more men within early childhood settings, which is a great move to redress the unequal balance within our profession. However, "This has resulted in an increased emphasis on the inappropriateness of touch" (Piper and Smith, 2003: 881). This is not a new problem – as this quote from nearly 25 years ago shows: "At first it was gay men who were under suspicion. Then, suddenly, it was all men working in the field. Now women are discouraged – even prevented – from holding children on their laps or helping them in the bathroom" (Tobin, 1997, p. 7).

Tobin raised the issue that suspicion and fear was spreading and inappropriately ruling in our settings and, sadly, from my own anecdotal research, this is still true today. Educators I meet have shared concern about how their loving interactions or positive touch will be interpreted by others, including their employers and many people have talked about feeling under suspicion due to their gender or sexuality. This is unfair and inappropriate and needs to be eradicated from practice. Yes, we need to safeguard children, but we need to do so without making any discriminatory assumptions about the adults who work with them. Francesco explains how he has responded and not let this stigma get in the way of him developing a loving pedagogy in his practice:

Francesco Mauro, a cultural perspective from a man in childcare

Prior to working in the UK, I worked for about two years in the educational field as a TA type of figure in a Forest School and Montessori school in Norway and in a Montessori school in Malta. It was interesting to note how the role of a man, within the educational setting, is perceived and treated in different ways. In Norway, based on my experience and the opinions of my colleagues at the time, seeing a man in a reception class, even though still rare, is normal and considered necessary for the adequate development of the pupils. Therefore, seeing a man cuddling one of the children after they hurt themselves or felt sad, was encouraged. In Malta seeing a man in a reception class is almost unheard of. Despite this I worked, successfully, with a wide range of pupils, taking care of babies up to six years old.

As an early years teacher, I believe that adequate and thought out physical contact sometimes works a lot better than spoken words. Young children don't have the cognitive structures in order to fully grasp what we are trying to communicate with them, but hugs are universal and, in some cases, a lot more effective than uninterrupted conversation. That is why, regardless of the cultural context surrounding me, I always made sure that my children received the physical contact they needed from me, regardless of my gender. I have no problems hugging, holding hands, or cuddling children until they fall asleep and I'll happily do that because that is one of the ways that, as an educator, I express how much I care for them.

Some parents are not always comfortable with the idea of having a grown man cuddling their child, but it is important to fight against the stigma, instead of getting offended, and demonstrating that everything is okay and I'm taking care of all aspects of their child's development. For instance, when I was working in Malta, there was one girl who didn't feel comfortable with me. Her mother was also really worried about having a man in the classroom and kept on asking questions regarding my practice to other colleagues, making sure I was doing the right thing. Even though it was upsetting at first, I decided to calmly address the situation with the mother, making sure she had all the answers she needed from me. The mother quickly warmed up to me and this transferred to the daughter, with whom I developed a good relationship from that day on.

Within my small research study, the educators observed were not afraid to demonstrate their affection for the children through touch. For example, they openly held the children's hands, welcomed children to sit on their laps, or comfortably rubbed suncream into their skin. Positive touch was encouraged both within policy and practice and my study suggested that the tactile interactions are evidence of love in action.

An example of adults naturally touching children occurred one hot day when I observed Sarah applying suncream to Beth's body (see Beth's story, below). This could be an uncomfortable time for both Sarah and Beth, as it involves rubbing cream into Beth's arms, legs and face. As an adult observing this interaction first hand, neither adult nor child look or appear to feel uncomfortable, in fact, the opposite is true. This becomes an intimate time where Beth receives some positive one-to-one adult attention and shares a joke with Sarah. This observation is in stark contrast to Piper and Smith's comment that, "The touching of children in professional settings is no longer relaxed, or instinctive" (2003: 891) as this interaction appeared to be both of these things. They continue that touch has become a, "self-conscious negative act" and educators are "controlled more by fear than by caring" (Piper and Smith, 2003: 891). However, my own research suggests that this is not always the case. Both Sarah and Beth enjoy the interaction and this natural positive act demonstrated the warm and affectionate relationship that they shared. Educators can stand firm on their loving pedagogy and sensitively and instinctively use touch to enhance their interactions with children.

Beth's story, Widcome Acorns: applying suncream

Sarah was one of the adults in the outside area during free-play time on a very hot day. The preschool has permission to apply sun cream to the children as appropriate.

Sarah asks three-year-old Beth, "Have you had suncream on today?"

Beth replies, "No."

Sarah, "OK – we need to do your suncream. Put your arms out like a robot!"

Sarah crouches down in front of Beth and squeezes some cream onto her hand. Beth laughs and happily puts both arms out straight in front of her and says in robot voice – "I - am- a- ro - bot!"

Sarah, "Can I rub it in?"

Sarah gently applies cream to Beth's arms and legs. Beth looks comfortable being touched by Sarah, and she starts giggling and laughing.

Sarah, "Is it tickling?"

Beth nods and giggles again, Sarah says, "You are really ticklish!"

Sarah continues smoothing cream onto Beth's arms and legs, finishing with her face.

Sarah, "Look up for a bit, that'll do."

Beth happily returns to her play.

Asking children for permission to touch them can also be a helpful safeguard too. For example, if children learn that adults, even parents, should ask before touching them, especially during intimate care, they will be more likely to recognise an inappropriate touch if an adult did not ask. So it can be sensible practice for a parent to ask their child during bath time, "Can I wash your hair?" or "Can I use the sponge to wash your bottom?" This is similar to teaching children the PANTS underwear rule, an initiative started by the National Society for the Prevention of Cruelty to Children (NSPCC, 2020) in order to keep children safe from sexual abuse:

P – Privates are private

A – Always remember your body belongs to you

N – No means no

T – Talk about secrets that upset you

S – Speak up, someone can help

Snapdragons Nurseries: policy promoting safe practice with regard to physical touch

Our policy explains that children in our care deserve to be in a secure, loving environment and physical contact should be open and initiated by the child's needs, eg for a hug when upset or help with toileting. We always prompt children to carry out personal care themselves and, if they cannot manage, ask if they would like help. We do not kiss children on the lips.

As part of the senior team, we would be delivering the message that all the children in our care need love, nurture and affection and, if they are giving a child a cuddle, it's done in the open, not hidden, and we acknowledge it, saying, "Oh that's nice you want a cuddle from me."

We also remind staff that for some children physical affection might be difficult, due to past experiences, or sensory issues etc. Affection for them can happen in a different way and on their terms. This could be a thumbs up, smile, or through words. The most important thing is that it is on the child's terms. All staff need to know what each child's 'comfort zone' is.

Nurturing touch

Touch is not just something that we are doing as part of our routine but it is also a powerful, nurturing force. So we can reflect upon how we use touch with children to promote their emotional wellbeing and begin to change the way we routinely interact with them physically. Let us take the example of changing nappies, which is an essential part of our role as educator to young children, not least because of the smell!

Changing nappies, a new father's perspective

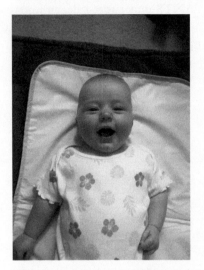

I have a clear memory of the first nappy I put on a baby. My oldest daughter was newly born, and while her mother lay exhausted on the birthing trolley, she greeted the world with a sticky poo of dark black meconium. I wiped her bottom, talking to her all the while about all the new things she was seeing around her, and wrapped her up, warm and dry.

Nappy changing may be smelly, but it is a blessed relief for the child, who starts off feeling sticky and uncomfortable, and ends up feeling clean and fresh. It is also a great opportunity to talk.

I used to talk with my children about all sorts. Sometimes we'd discuss the merits of the new washable nappies we'd bought, other times I'd compliment them on their colourful romper suits. Smiles and gurgles were all I got in reply, but they certainly meant something to my babies. It was the perfect opportunity for a tickle on the tummy, or even kisses and raspberries, while their favourite toy looked on from the edge of the changing mat. We chatted about what we had been doing that morning, and what our plans were for the rest of the day (I always thought it good to keep them informed). I practised my baby signing, especially the signs for 'dirty' and 'clean', which reinforced their own language development. As they grew, they started to copy these signs themselves!

Then the poppers were done up, and it was up in the air they went. Wheee! I flew them back to the playmat, or the highchair, or whatever it was they were doing.

Before I had children I imagined that nappy changing would be a smelly, dirty task to be put up with. Little did I know how much fun it could be.

We can approach the routine of nappy changing as just that, a job that needs to be accomplished as quickly as possible, or we can see it as a moment for nurturing the child and building our relationship. This is good quality 1:1 time with them and an opportunity to deepen our bond. For example we can tickle their toes or pull funny faces to make them laugh. We can talk gently to them explaining that we need to change their nappy, then chat about what we are doing and why or sing a changing nappy song, making and sustaining eye contact during the special time. Changing a dirty nappy also helps the child to feel more comfortable so it will have a soothing effect. Thinking about times in our routine when we can use touch in a special way to nurture our children is an essential part of developing a loving pedagogy.

In discussion with Sonia Mainstone-Cotton, positive touch

I work as a nurture consultant with four-year-old children in their reception year, all of whom have social, emotional and mental health difficulties. Positive touch is an important part of supporting a child in an emotionally rich and nurturing way. We know that the words we use with children are important, as well the way we smile with our whole face as this is showing warmth and love to children. Alongside this, gentle physical touch can also be a hugely calming and nurturing experience for some children.

If I am with a child who is emotionally struggling, they may be shouting, crying or hiding, so as well as recognising and validating their feelings by naming them, I also gently stroke their arm or their back or sometimes their hair, in a gentle and calming way. Many children find this comforting and calming. By using this gentle touch I am also sharing my own calmness and my calm breathing, to help them in their regulation.

When children are becoming overwhelmed they need help in reconnecting and they need help in finding a way to soothe and find a sense of calm. Young children are unable to do this by themselves; they need calm and regulated adults to support them. We often think of soothing babies via touch when they are distressed but we don't always think of using this with older children. I had one little girl I worked with for whom life was extremely frightening. When she became distressed her key worker would scoop her up and rock her, like she was a baby. She would sit and rock and sometimes gently sing to the girl, and would use words to reassure that she was safe and loved. The gentle touch through being held and the rocking movement always helped to soothe this little girl.

It's important that we know the children we are working with, knowing their individual likes and preferences, one child I work with responds well to his back being gently rubbed, another child I work with hates this, but enjoys having hand cream massaged into her hands. It's important we take our cues from the children; they will let us know what works and doesn't work for them.

Many children will need to return to our side during the day for a cuddle or to hold our hand. If you relate this to attachment theory, children may need reassurance if they feel overwhelmed, worried, tired or frightened. Research has shown that caregiver touch positively impacts children's emotional development and their ability to respond to fear or anxiety (Thrasher and Grossmann, 2019). Therefore we should build times into our day when we can recharge their batteries or refill their emotional tank and offer them the comfort they need. We must be available and ensure that we never turn a child away and plan to have nurture times written into our routine.

Charlotte Proctor, using physical touch

When I was working as an early years practitioner, using physical touch was a grey area. There was one little girl, aged two, who was always very upset when she left her mum in the morning. She came in everyday emotionally distressed and needed a hug and a story. At first I was hesitant to approach the child in a loving, comforting way because I was new and did not know the boundaries that the preschool had in place – whether it was ok to pick children up and cuddle them when they are emotionally distressed. I asked another practitioner if she could help me and I'll observe what to do. This observation helped me to know how to handle this situation in the future. I became confident in my approach to situations that require professional love.

It is really important that we get to know our children really well so that we can respond in the moment as sensitively as possible. I observed a skilled teacher comforting a child who had been told off in the playground by a different adult and was struck by how she instinctively crouched at the child's level and gently rubbed the child's back as she talked in a soothing voice. She was able to calm the little girl down but she also reinforced what had been said and turned the situation around so that it ended up with them both smiling and laughing. The teacher clearly had a good relationship with the girl and knew how to sensitively respond.

Sally Kirkby, Headington Quarry

I remember a child asking me, "Mrs Kirkby, please can I have a cuddle?" She sat on my lap, we had a cuddle then she freely got down and continued to play. This sort of thing happens regularly and I try to make sure that I am available to the children if they need me.

In summary

Most children will want and need physical contact and touch in order to feel safe, secure and loved and it is up each individual setting to consider what is appropriate positive touch and each educator to set their own specific boundaries. Obviously being physically tactile with children raises safeguarding issues. However, we should not allow this to prevent us from using appropriate touch with children. My own research highlighted that not all adults are fearful about using caring touch, which is evidence of a loving pedagogy in practice. Therefore, we need to openly discuss this in our settings and be really clear in our policies about how we will use touch to demonstrate love. Then we can stand firm on our loving pedagogy, knowing that research backs up the view that caring touch is a vital component of young children's development.

Questions for reflection

1. To what extent have you discussed with colleagues about how you will interact physically with the children in your care and demonstrate love through touch?

2. What could you say that would reassure parents about any safeguarding concerns they may have?

3. How can you build nurture times into your day and ensure that there are regular opportunities for physical interaction and touch?

References

All-Party Parliamentary Group on a Fit and Healthy Childhood (APPG) (2020). *Wellbeing and Nurture: Physical and Emotional Security in Childhood* Retrieved from https://fhcappg.org.uk/wp-content/uploads/2020/07/ReportWellbeingandNurtureFinal140720.pdf.

Aslanian, T. (2018). Embracing uncertainty: a diffractive approach to love in the context of early childhood education and care. *International Journal of Early Years Education*, *26*(2), 173–185.

Bergnehr, D. and Cekaite, A. (2018). Adult-initiated touch and its functions at a Swedish preschool: controlling, affectionate, assisting and educative haptic conduct. *International Journal of Early Years Education*, *26*(3), 312–331.

Byrne, J. (2016). Love in social care: necessary pre-requisite or blurring of boundaries. *Scottish Journal of Residential Child Care*, *15*(3), 152–158.

Coffey, H. (2020). Affection deprivation: what happens to our bodies when we go without touch? *Independent*, 8 May. Retrieved from. www.independent.co.uk/life-style/touch-skin-hunger-hugs-coronavirus-lockdown-isolation-ctactile-afferent-nerve-a9501676.html.

Mainstone-Cotton, S. (2017). *Promoting Young Children's Emotional Health and Wellbeing: A Practical Guide for Professionals and Parents*. London: Jessica Kingsley Publishers.

McGlone, F., Wessberg, J. and Olausson, H. (2014). Discriminative and affective touch: sensing and feeling. *Neuron, 82*(4), 737–755.

von Mohr, M., Kirsch, L.P. and Fotopoulou, A. (2017). The soothing function of touch: affective touch reduces feelings of social exclusion. *Scientific Reports 7,* 13516.

NSPCC (2020). www.nspcc.org.uk/keeping-children-safe/support-for-parents/pants-under wear-rule/.

Okruszek, L., Aniszewska-Stańczuk, A., Piejka, A., Wiśniewska, M. and Żurek, K., (2020). Safe but lonely? Loneliness, mental health symptoms and COVID-19. Pre-print retrieved from https://psyarxiv.com/9njps/.

Piper, H. and Smith, H. (2003). 'Touch' in educational and child care settings: dilemmas and responses. *British Educational Research Journal, 29*(6), 879–894.

Thrasher C. and Grossmann T. (2019). Children's emotion perception in context: the role of caregiver touch and relationship quality emotion. *American Psychological Association.* Retrieved from https://pubmed.ncbi.nlm.nih.gov/31750706/.

Tobin, J. (1997). *Making a Place for Pleasure in Early Childhood Education.* New Haven, CT: Yale University Press.

Tuulari, J., Scheinin, N., Lehtola, S., Merisaari, H., Saunavaara, J., Parkkola, R., Sehlstedt, I., Karlsson, L., Karlsson, H. and Björnsdotter, M. (2019). Neural correlates of gentle skin stroking in early infancy. *Developmental Cognitive Neuroscience, 35*, 36–41.

5 The language(s) of love – love in practice

Introduction

Chapman and Campbell (2012) have identified five main love languages (physical touch, words of affirmation, acts of service, quality time and gifts) and they propose that everyone has a preferred way of loving and feeling loved, their own love languages if you like. For example, if a child is constantly told by their mother, "I love you" but their mother rarely spends time with them, if their primary language is 'quality time' they are unlikely to feel loved. Likewise, if a parent prefers not to kiss and cuddle their child, even if they spend lots of time with their child, if the child's preferred way to receive love is through physical touch, they may feel unloved.

I am considering these ideas in the context of early years because if practitioners understand how their key children prefer to be loved, they will better understand how to relate to them and will do so more appropriately, which in turn will enable these children to feel loved. And when a child feels loved, they will be more secure and learn more effectively. This chapter draws upon these ideas, explores each of these languages in turn and considers how we can use this approach within early childhood settings to support children.

The theory around love languages

Chapman's initial work around love languages, called *The 5 Love Languages: The Secret to Love that Lasts* (1992) was aimed at couples and focused on helping each partner better understand the other. Chapman received many requests to link this idea with children in terms of a parent–child relationship and joined up with his friend Campbell who, as the author of *How to Really Love Your Child* (1977), was well placed to consider the love languages in relation to children. Together they wrote *The 5 Love Languages of Children*

(2012) which outlines how to find out your child's love language and how to make them feel loved.

The idea is that everyone prefers to give and receive love in certain ways and finding out the love language that your children prefer will enable you to express love in a way they understand. They state: "By speaking your child's own love language, you can fill his 'emotional tank' with love" (Chapman and Campbell, 2012: 17). This metaphor of an 'emotional tank' reminds me of the importance of nurturing children and focusing on their wellbeing. It is sometimes easy to overlook our children's emotional development as we focus on more academic things, yet supporting children emotionally lays the foundation for other sorts of learning. Developing a loving pedagogy and keeping the child and individual in mind will ensure that their emotional wellbeing takes a high priority.

Read (2014) discusses love in practice when considering how to promote secure attachments in young children. Practical ideas such as creating cosy corners for children to cuddle up in and listen to a story are suggested and attention is also given to the creation of special nurture time which Goldschmied and Jackson (2004: 46) refer to as an "island of intimacy" when a child can have time and space to emotionally refuel. Such nurture times should be an essential part of our daily routine as children need time and space to relax and remain or regain feelings of calmness. Reflecting upon children's love languages will ensure that nurture and wellbeing are central to our provision.

Chapman and Freed (2015) extend this concept into the educational field providing lesson plans and practical guidelines for teachers, believing that understanding these love languages will positively impact learning. However, they focus on children aged over seven, and considering love as a language has not been researched into in depth with younger children. I believe that it could act as an additional lens through which to view professional love and a helpful way of observing loving relationships. These books about love languages are not aimed at kindergarten or preschool-aged children; however, they could easily be adapted in a more developmentally appropriate way to younger children and, if we consider how our children prefer to give and receive love, we can build better attachments and enable them to feel safe and secure. There is a considerable overlap with themes from Reggio Emilia, a child-centered approach stemming from a city in northern Italy, that incorporates the idea that a child discovers the world through a hundred different languages. Loving is included within the list that Malaguzzi shares in the poem *The Child is Made of One Hundred* (Edwards, Gandini and Forman, 2012). This acknowledges the multitude of ways that children can express their feelings and experiences. Perhaps from a child's perspective love is simply one form of meaningful expression.

Klein (1989) studied children aged between two and a half and six years with a view to finding out how young children understood the concept of love. The study suggests that young children think they love others at specific times. Physical proximity to those they love is important and hugging and kissing was one of the main ways that young children understood the concept of love. However, as the children grew older other factors materialised, such as friendship, spending time together or playing together. Thus Klein proposed that young children do have a reasonable understanding of what love means in the context of relationships.

Although the term love languages may be new to many people, it is generally accepted that loving implies more than just emotion and includes action of some sort (see Chapter 1), and love languages are about acting in natural ways that keep someone's best interests at heart. I believe these ideas to be deep rooted within society and culture, as people demonstrate their love for one another in many different ways. We will now explore each love language in more detail and I encourage you to reflect upon your provision as you read to consider if any of your children speak each language and how you cater for them. In addition to other case studies, Pebbles childcare have kindly give me illustrations of each love language and are covered in this chapter.

Physical touch

This language is about children who want to be cuddled, hugged or held and want to cuddle, hug and hold others – for example, a child who sits on your lap, holds your hand, strokes your back, or snuggles into you during a story. Offering children positive physical touch makes them feel wanted, loved and helps to build a secure attachment. Klein's study found that children recognised love through physical interactions stating, "All young children viewed hugging and kissing as expressions of love" (Klein, 1989: 27).

When I was teaching, I can remember one particular child who would always want to sit on my lap or near me on the carpet and stroke my leg! At the time I did not know anything about love languages but, reflecting upon this now, I realise that this little girl's love language was probably physical touch. Some children crave more physical attention than others and we need to ensure that our routines and interactions allow lots of touch, for example, including touch as an option when greeting children or saying goodbye.

Greetings pillar, Lechlade Little Learners

A member of staff had a great idea for a greetings pillar. The idea is children can choose how greetings are exchanged on arrival and departure. So we wrote on some log slices different greetings and attached them to a pillar near the door. The children love pointing to the different pictures and choosing how to be greeted!

Chapter 4 has thought in detail about the tactile nature of a loving pedagogy and encouraged us to reflect upon the level of physical contact we permit in our settings. It argued that touch is essential for all children and our setting's policies should acknowledge this. It is vital that all educators consider this area and decide as a team what our approach will be.

The language of touch, Pebbles Childcare

Physical touch is essential to children's emotional growth and development and in developing secure relationships. As a setting, we cuddle the children, kiss their 'hurts', hold hands on walks and adventures, they sit on our laps and snuggle as they watch a movie and we feel able to respond their emotional needs using physical touch in various forms, just as their parents would. As we care for younger babies, sometimes all they need is to be held and cuddled, especially when teething or settling. We don't need any excuses to sit, cuddle and share a book.

Physical touch may not always be cuddles and hugs. Some children really like to rough and tumble or have a horsey-ride on the back of an adult and lots of children would appreciate a high five or fist bump. Lots of games that we play are contact sports and so playing ball games together can also be a way of combining quality time with physical touch. In addition, there are times when physical touch might be more important than others. For example, if a child is hurt, upset or feeling ill, or when a child is feeling very tired, we can help them to feel better using gentle positive touch.

There are naturally times in our routine when touch is more prevalent too, for example holding hands when walking together, sitting on a lap while listening to a story or helping a child to get dressed. We can use these times to demonstrate our love and seek other opportunities, for example by gently squeezing a child's shoulder as we walk past them or ruffling their hair. We need to remain attuned to our children to ensure that we read their signals correctly and, if a child appears to dislike our touch, winces or pulls away, we must immediately stop. Therefore, observation is key to understanding which children have a love language of touch and which do not.

All children need a basic level of physical touch and so if we notice that a child we look after craves more physical touch than others, we can:

- Always greet them by getting down to their level with a hug or other positive touch. (Make sure that other watching children do not feel left out, as several children may have more than one preferred language.)

- Allow them to cuddle up or sit on your lap during a story.

■ Comfort them with a cuddle if they are tired or upset.

■ Offer them a 'high five' or gently squeeze their shoulder when praising them.

■ Gain their attention using their name while gently touching their arm.

■ Play games that require physical touch like circle games (holding hands), rough and tumble or clapping games.

■ Offer them positive touch throughout the day, for example massage their back/shoulders, rub lotion into their hands or engage in a 'thumb-war' for fun!

Words of affirmation

Some children respond more than others to verbal praise and encouragement. For example, we may see a child glow with pride when we praise their contribution. Offering words of affirmation to a child makes them feel proud, worthy and valued.

Are we listening to children and the words they use? If children express their love using words, they will feel more loved if they hear words back that demonstrate love to them. For example, my youngest child said to her daddy, "I love you down to your feet" and she has always enjoyed stories involving love. She likes us to tell her that we love her; it helps her to feel loved. She is also very tactile so, for her, hearing "I love you" while being cuddled is a double whammy!

Sally Kirkby, Headington Quarry Foundation Stage School

We need to listen to our children and value what they say. One particular child regularly expressed her love using words, saying things like:

> "Briony, I love you"
> "I love you when I'm at home and when I'm at school. I love you when I'm on holiday and when it's Eid"

We need to reflect upon the way we use language. Are we encouraging children in what we say to them? Do we label praise, for example, saying, "Wow I love the way you just jumped with two feet together!" This not only commends that child for their action but also informs them of what they achieved that was so good, and relates this to their behaviour not their person. In contrast, saying, "Good girl" or "Good boy" can be empty praise as it is not formative and could leave the child feeling unsure about why they are good. I saw a funny example of this when I was observing a student in a school. The class teacher was trying to encourage all the children to sit on the carpet and she said, "Good boy" to four-year-old George who was already sitting down. What the teacher did not see was that George was sitting there picking his nose and she had just praised him for that! I asked George what he had done that was good and he said, "I dunno, I'm just picking my nose!"

This beautiful message was left by my friend's daughter to her daddy on the floor in the garage. She has made it out of screws and nails!
   She was expressing her love through words.

It is vital that we think about how we use language on a day-to-day basis with young children and how they hear us using language with each other. We are probably very careful not to swear in the presence of a child; however, how many times have we been self-critical or sarcastic. We may not view this use of language to be problematic; however, children are always watching and listening to what we say and what we do. If we are regularly self-critical, they may learn to be critical of themselves, which could have a very negative impact on their self-esteem. For example, if we are at the mark-making table with a few children, it is very easy for our insecurities to creep in. and for us to say something like, "I know it doesn't look like a unicorn, I'm not very good at drawing." This is inadvertently giving children the message that there is a right way to draw a unicorn and is instilling the opposite to the can-do attitude we try so hard to promote.

   If we use sarcasm, the joke will be lost on the children as very young children tend to take comments literally and not understand the subtleties of sarcastic wit. Often sarcasm is at the expense another person and is used to deliberately put someone, or even ourselves, down. It often literally says the opposite from what is meant which will be very confusing for young children. Sarcasm is not appropriate for children to hear and we should avoid using it in our settings as we would avoid expletives.

Using words, Pebbles Childcare

Words are really important to us and this love language is fluid throughout our practice, providing positive affirmation to our children throughout the day and as they go about their play and learning. We've found that by labelling praise for the children their sense of self and self-worth develops, which, in turn, develops their confidence in their own abilities and in themselves as a person and member of the group. For example, narrating a child's behaviour saying something like, "You're splashing your feet in the water, splish, splash, splosh!" would encourage the child to continue this action.

I grew up hearing the chant, "Sticks and stones may break my bones but words will never hurt me" but it is simply not true. Words are very powerful and can easily hurt or make a person feel small, insignificant and unloved. So we need to be very careful how we use language in our settings and ensure that we only use words to build self-esteem and confidence and never use them to deliberately hurt a child.

As they grow older, children will also be able to express their love through written words and language and you may find that they will like nothing better than to write little notes and cards for the people they love. One child wrote this letter to her friend when she had just turned five years old and she loved to write notes to friends and family. I understand that language has remained very important to her as she has grown up. I wonder if, when older, children who have a love language of words will be wooed by a love letter or poetry!

If we recognise words of affirmation as one of our children's love languages we can:

■ Cheer them on in games and verbally encourage them when they try to achieve things.

■ Tell them that they are special and regularly use words of endearment and affection towards them.

■ Verbally praise their efforts and actions by labelling the praise, for example, "Wow, I love the colours you have chosen!" or "Giving Ben your toy was really kind."

■ Make a point of telling another member of staff how you are proud of the child in their hearing.

■ When parents arrive to collect, verbally praise the child to their parent, for example, "Sanya built such a tall tower today, it was amazing!"

■ Use encouraging words with children, for example, "You can do it!" or "I like the way you shared your bike with Sarah. Taking it in turns is a great way to play with a friend."

■ Explain to them that it is OK to make mistakes and value every contribution they make, regardless of their levels of success.

■ Write notes to the children containing words of encouragement.

■ Leave messages with hearts in the outdoor area for their children to find.

■ If a child gives you a picture/note, value it and tell them how precious it is to you.

■ Take photographs of their creations or pictures and display them with messages stating why they are so valued in your setting.

Lunctime messages

As a parent, leaving messages in lunch boxes is a great way of telling our children that we love them, even when we are not there.

Acts of service

The love language of acts of service describes children who like to do things for others and enjoy having things done for them. For example, a child who offers to help you or who is thrilled when you offer to get them their shoes or coat. We are often teaching children to be independent, However, in order to feel loved and cared for, some children want to be physically looked after through acts of service. It is something like when we enjoy going to an all-inclusive hotel on holiday so that we do not have to cook, clean or run around after anyone else. Others are serving us for a change and it feels good.

According to Klein's research (1989), when asked about how they express their love for others, children discussed helping others; for example feeding a pet fits into the bracket of acts of service. Young children often enjoy helping and like to do things

for other people. I remember when my own children loved nothing more than to 'help' me with the washing or sweeping up. This links with the notion that children learn through imitation and we tend to want to imitate the people we admire, look up to or love.

So, although we want to encourage children to become independent, can we sometimes still do things for them as an act of service? It is not about allowing children to be lazy and us running around after their every whim! Those same children will probably happily do things for us in return. If a child has this love language, they will be the first to volunteer and will enjoy learning new skills that they can use to help others. From an adult perspective, imagine your friend has just moved house. They are perfectly capable of cooking their own dinner and unpacking themselves, but turning up with some pizzas and offering to help unpack might be a true demonstration of friendship. This self-less act of service shows your love.

In our settings we need to make sure that we are available for the children and are ready to help, even if they do not really need help. Sometimes just being there can demonstrate our love. For example, if my daughter is running late for school, I can get her bowl of cereal ready for her. She usually has to sort herself out, but by preparing her breakfast I am demonstrating my love and serving her. Knowing that she is short of time, she may even ask me to help, and by telling her to get her breakfast herself, if her love language is acts of service, it would act as a mini rejection. So it is important for us to know if a child loves in this way.

Sisterly love, Westview Day Nursery

During one session when Lyra was playing hop-scotch with her friends, her younger sister, Sophie, approached her. Lyra immediately included her, telling her the rules, holding her hand and walking her through. Although Sophie was not able to hop, Lyra was very encouraging saying, "It's OK if you jump". This was a real act of service for Sophie and demonstrated Lyra's love for her.

Acts of service can also be about holding children in mind and choosing a specific story because we know they will love it, or taking them to a certain place because we know they will be very interested. Perhaps they have previously brought us a broken toy, by the simple act of fixing it, we are showing that we care. This type of service can be physically and emotionally demanding and, in one sense, being a parent is an act of service that lasts for between 18 years and a lifetime! Acts of service are not about just doing things to please our children, instead they are about helping the child to feel loved, keeping their emotional tank topped up through serving them and being a role model. In one sense we need to be the person we want our children to grow up to be.

In search of puddles, a parent's perspective

My little boy was full of energy this morning and we were going to just stay in, but I suddenly thought, why not get him out of the house! He loves splashing in puddles (mummy not so much) so we thought we would go in search of some!

This parent, who knew that her son loves to splash in puddles, despite not enjoying it much herself, took him in search of some puddles. This is an example of an act of service, when we do something for a child because we know they will appreciate it.

Serving our children, Pebbles Childcare

This love language is particularly relevant for our current cohort of school leavers; they are an incredibly independent bunch and thrive on their independent play (developing and extending their own learning and play together, but without adult intervention or support). And so we frequently plan invitations to play, experiences and child-led opportunities that they can access independently, but that we know they will enjoy and will provide an adequate level of challenge. This enables them to feel like they've achieved something wonderful, all on their own. By planning this way we are serving the children.

Our children also serve each other as the older ones do things for the younger ones. This is part of the family dynamic we've tried to create as a setting.

If one of our children likes us to do things for them and we think their love language is acts of service we can:

■ Plan to do things specifically for them.

■ Ask them to help with tasks at several points during the day.

■ When a child asks for help, respond sensitively, decide if their emotional tank needs refuelling and, if it does, jump in to help!

■ Mend that toy that they have asked us to fix.

■ Sit next to a child to help them work through a problem or task.

■ Cook their favourite meal especially for them.

■ Occasionally set up their favourite toys, rather than always encouraging the child to get them out.

■ Make a list of their favourite activities and weave these into our weekly planning.

■ Create spaces for the children – cosy corners or dens furnished with their interests.

Quality time

Children whose main love language is quality time will want to spend time with you – for example a child who actively seeks out adult attention and wants to be near you in the setting. Spending quality time with a child tells them that they are important, we want to spend time with them and we love them.

Klein's study found that children saw spending time together and playing together as an expression of love (1989) and many parents would recognise the scenario of their child tugging at their sleeve or pestering them to come and play. Often educators describe some children as 'attention seeking', although it is my view that if a child is seeking our attention, as all behaviour is communication, this is a clear message! For the child, even negative attention is attention.

So when we look at attention-seeking behaviour, we need to question the aim of this behaviour. It is, of course, to gain our attention, love and to connect with us. Children who use attention-seeking behaviour need more attention and spending quality time with them is a good place to start. Give the child as much attention as possible when they are behaving appropriately and if they are behaving inappropriately, calmly ask them to stop; for example, "If you stop X we can go and play a game together." This offers them the attention that they want at the same time as discouraging the poor behaviour. If the child is seeking our attention at a time when we are busy, we need to explain why we are unable to come at that moment; for example, "I will come and look as soon as I have finished changing this nappy." If possible we could involve the child in what we are doing while they wait; for example, "Can you pass me the babywipes?"

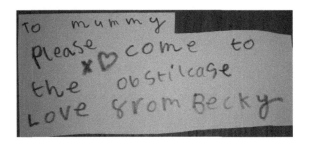

Of course, not all children who want to spend quality time with us will instigate it inappropriately. Some children will ask us to play or even write us notes to this end. My youngest daughter, Becky sent me this invitation, asking me to participate in an 'obstil case' (obstacle course) that she had set up.

Spending time together, Pebbles Childcare

Spending quality time with the children is something that is incredibly important to us and we feel really blessed to experience. As a smaller setting we focus on developing family values and a home-from-home ethos; the children's comments and opinions shape our setting effect-

ively – they shape what we do, when we do it and why we do it. They are in charge of their own learning and we do our best to facilitate their needs and interests with their comments and needs at the forefront of our practice.

Similarly, due to the family nature of our setting, we spend 1:1 time or small group time with our children, either sharing a snack or a drink and just chatting to them. In our opinion this displays to the children that we value them, we enjoy their company and we are interested in what they have to say and share with us.

Chapman and Campbell state:

> It's easier to give physical touch and words of affirmation than quality time. Few of us have enough hours in the day to get everything done as it is; giving a child quality time may mean that we have to give up something else.
>
> (2012: 64)

As an educator we have the luxury of what a parent does not have with their child: time. So it can help to reflect upon how we spend our time with our children. Do we spend 1:1 time with each child? Do we really listen to what children say and value their comments? Do we enjoy their company?

When we recognise that a child's love language is quality time we can:

- Plan in specific time to spend with them during the week.

- Include them in daily activities and organise rotas to enable them to be with adults frequently.

- Listen and respond to their attention-seeking behaviour; it means that they need more attention.

- Offer them undivided and focused attention in small groups or on a 1:1 basis.

- Share meals together and ask them about their interests and fascinations.

- Invite a child to read a story with you.

- Make eye contact with the children as they tell you important things.

- Have a specific place in the outside area that is your special place to be with each other.

- Play with them or alongside them just because you want to.

- Create photo books and reminisce about times we have spent together in the setting.

Gifts

This love language is about children who love to give and receive gifts and presents. This does not necessarily mean things that are bought or have monetary value. For example, bringing in some conkers to the setting is the perfect gift for a child we know is collecting them and a child who brings you a treasured stone in the garden and tells you that you can keep it is demonstrating their love to you. Offering children gifts in addition to other love languages can reinforce the idea that you care and hold them in mind.

Gifts for our children, Pebbles Childcare

In our setting we have a 'Pebbles Point' system whereby children can be awarded a point when we witness kindness, helpfulness, a particular skill or achievement. Once the child has collected ten points, we go out and buy them a magazine on a topic that we know they are interested in. Similarly, when resourcing our setting on our weekend trips to the charity shop, we often buy certain resources with specific children in mind. For example, one of our children has shown an increasing interest in more difficult puzzles and so we bought her a number of tricky puzzles, which she is able to sit down and do independently while the other children nap, and we store these separately to the playroom puzzles to allow her to continue where she left off if she loses interest or runs out of time before she completes it.

Sometimes gifts can be given to substitute for not spending quality time with a child or as a reward for something, and this would make them empty and not a meaningful expression of love. Chapman and Campbell suggest that other love languages must be given alongside gifts in order for the gift to express the love behind the gesture (2012). These gifts are not payment or rewards for doing something; they are freely given as an expression of love and should be undeserved. There is a difference between an adult giving a child something, in return for something else, or just giving for the sake of giving. For example, if I say to a child, "If you tidy the toys you can have a sticker", this is rewarding the tidying with a sticker and is not a true gift. Whereas if I know that Johnny loves stickers and I present him with one, without linking it to his behaviour, this is a true gift. This links with the idea of unconditional love which is discussed in Chapter 6.

Sourcing new resources, a preschool's perspective

Jasmine loved the Disney film *Frozen*. So when her key person sourced some characters from the film to include in small world play, Jasmine was over the moon! This is an example of how we can appropriately share gifts with the children in our care.

As educators, one way that we can give gifts to children is to create resources for them. An example of this is the visual timetable created for James in Chapter 7. One practitioner I spoke to created a special game designed around the child's interests and they loved it so much she had to make a second one, so that the child had one for in nursery and one for home!

Sally Kirkby, Headington Quarry Foundation Stage School

I can remember a child who used to look at me with love in her eyes. She regularly brought things to me and used to say, "I love Sally so much!" Bringing things to me was the way she used to show her love.

If gifts is their love language, allowing children to collect things will enable them to feel loved. If we say, "No you can't keep it", it dismisses their desire and gives them the message that their interests do not matter. I have had to struggle with this one myself, as my youngest child is a collector, aka a hoarder! When she was a little younger I asked her why she picks up every stick and stone she sees, and she told me that she *had* to because they speak to her and ask to be collected and if she does not pick them up they will feel lonely and will feel like she does not love them, which she clearly does!

If we think that one of our children appreciates gifts we can:

■ Hold the child in mind and make resources specifically for them.

■ Pick a daisy or collect a shiny stone from the garden and offer it to them.

■ Bring back a shell from the beach at the weekend as a gift for them.

■ Value the 'treasures' that they give us; for example, put that feather on display!

■ Use tangible rewards with them alongside labelled praise.

■ Follow their interests and plan activities that specifically cater for them.

■ Present the child with a special mealtime as a gift to them, make their favourite food, make the table look special too, as if you were in a posh restaurant!

■ Wrap up any new toys or resources and present them to the group as a gift.

■ Pop to the charity shop and pick up a little something that you know the child will adore.

- If we need to buy any new resources for the setting, allow the children to help us choose.

- Pay attention to the child as they receive their gifts, making eye contact and take the time to watch them enjoy the gifts.

Working out our children's love languages

In order to find out the love languages of our children we may need to do a little detective work. Firstly, we need to observe them, actively listen and become attuned to their different personalities and characteristics. As Chapman and Campbell note, "Young children are just beginning to learn how to receive and express love in the various languages" (2012: 111). They mention that love languages are not fixed and children might go through stages in loving, appearing to prefer one language at one stage and another at a later date. So we need to remain flexible, vigilant and keep observing and talking to our children to ascertain their main love language. They also recommend helping children to, "give and receive love in all the languages" (Chapman and Campbell, 2012: 112). This is crucial because over the course of their lives they will meet people with different love languages and the more fluently they speak in each language, the more socially adept they will become. Therefore, if we find our children have a preferred language, it is important for us not to neglect the other four. In addition, this chapter has focused on the five described by Chapman and Campbell. However, there could be more languages than this, so keep an open mind when observing how your children prefer to give and receive love.

Chapman and Campbell suggest five methods to help us discover our children's primary love languages:

1. Observe how they express love to their parent.
2. Observe how they express love to you or others.
3. Listen to the requests that the child make.
4. Notice what they complain about.
5. Offer opportunities for a child to choose between two languages and notice what they choose.

(2012: 113–115)

Children often express love in the way in which they most want to receive, so observing how they express their love to their parents or to other people can give us a clue as to their primary love language. For example, if a child is always wanting to hold your hand and cuddle you, you can assume their primary language is 'physical touch'; or if a child regularly gives you compliments or tells you they love you, it would be fair to assume their primary language is 'words of affirmation'. If a child wants to help you all the time they might fit better into the 'acts of service' language, or if a child does not leave your side, perhaps it is about spending 'quality time' together; and, lastly, if a child often gives you flowers, stones, or things they have found, perhaps their primary language is 'gifts'.

You can also actively listen to the child and the things they ask for or complain about. Sometimes children ask us to read them a story or to watch them on the swings and this implies that 'quality time' is important to them. Other children might seek reassurance through words asking you what you think of their picture implying 'words of affirmation', while others still might complain that they have not had a hug from you yet today, which is indicating that 'physical touch' is their main language.

Chapman and Campbell's fifth method asks the child to choose between two languages, for example between quality time or a gift and noting what the child chooses. If these choices are noted down, over time, a pattern will emerge and we can work out which language they prefer. They have some simple questionnaires that can be used and some ideas of choices; for example, "Would you rather wrestle (physical touch) or read a story together (Quality time)?, When I am out of town for two days, would you rather I bring you a present (gift) or send you a special email (words of affirmation)?" (Chapman and Campbell, 2012: 116). Their ideas are based around the parent–child relationship and focus on children aged between 6 and 15 years old. I have had a go at writing my own ideas about appropriate choices for younger children.

Using choices to discover the love language with preschool aged children: (Inspired by Chapman and Campbell, 2012)

- Would you rather I give you a high five (physical touch) or I tell mummy you helped me today (words of affirmation)?
- I have a few minutes spare; shall I fix that broken toy that you asked for (acts of service) or make you a special card (words of affirmation)?
- Shall I go and find you flower from outside (gifts) or shall we play outside together (quality time)?
- As a thank you for tidying up, would you like this feather I have found (gifts) or shall I write you a thank you note (words of affirmation)?
- Shall I sit next to you at the table (quality time) or shall I make you your favourite meal (acts of service)?
- Shall we have a tickling fight (physical touch) or shall we play this game together (quality time)?
- Would you like to sit on my lap (physical touch) or would you prefer me to find you a special sticker to take home (gifts)?

- Shall I put your picture on the wall with a note saying how fantastic it is (words of affirmation) or shall we make another picture together (quality time)?
- Shall I find you a superhero toy (gifts) or shall I create a superhero den (acts of service)?
- Would you like me to help you put your shoes on (acts of service) or do you want to sit on my lap while you put your own shoes on (physical touch)?

Of course, with lots of these choices, as you are trying to ascertain what the child thinks, once you have worked this out, there is nothing to stop you doing both choices anyway!

An important point to raise at the end of this chapter is that if we identify specific love languages in our children, we must never use these languages to express hostility or our anger. For example, if we refuse to cuddle a child whose love language is physical touch, this will be devastating for them and the ultimate rejection. Likewise, if we use words to condemn or criticise a child and their love language is words of affirmation, the words can hurt more than ever.

In summary

Children, we all in fact, like to give and receive love in different ways. It can be quite helpful to reflect upon ourselves and how we feel loved or demonstrate our love for others. For example, would I prefer to receive a bouquet of flowers (gifts) or for someone to make me breakfast in bed (acts of service) or perhaps I would prefer to have an evening out with my loved one. Then I need to think about those closest to me and reflect upon how they might prefer to receive my love. That way I can ensure that my love is received in the spirit in which it was sent!

This chapter has explored the five love languages outlined by Chapman and Campbell (2012): physical touch, words of affirmation, acts of service, quality time and gifts. It has shared the theory around love languages and offered ideas of how to adapt our provision to suit each of these languages. So we need to try to work out our children's main love languages and then adjust our provision in order to fill their emotional tanks with love.

Questions for reflection

1. What makes you feel loved – can you identify your own main love language?

2. What impact will speaking your children's love languages have on their self-esteem and behaviour?

3. How can adults speak children's 'love languages' more fluently?

References

Campbell, R. (1977). *How to Really Love Your Child*. Wheaton, IL: Victor Books.

Chapman, G. (1992). *The 5 Love Languages: The Secret to Love that Lasts*. Chicago, IL: Northfield Publishing.

Chapman, G. and Campbell, R. (2012). *The 5 Love Languages of Children*. Chicago, IL: Northfield Publishing.

Chapman, G. and Freed, D. (2015). *Discovering the 5 Love Languages at School*. Chicago, IL: Northfield Publishing.

Edwards, C., Gandini, L. and Forman, G. (2012). *The Hundred Languages of Children: The Reggio Emilia Experience in Transformation*, 3rd edn. California: Praeger.

Goldschmied, E. and Jackson, S. (2004). *People Under Three: Young Children in Daycare*, 2nd edn. London: Routledge.

Klein, P. (1989). Young children's understanding of love. *International Journal of Early Childhood, 21*(1), 27–34.

Read, V. (2014). *Developing Attachment in Early Years Settings: Nurturing Secure Relationships from Birth to Five Years,* 2nd edn. Abingdon: Routledge.

6 The empowerment of children through love

Introduction

Children are living in a world where they have very little power. Their lives are planned to the *n*th degree and they do not have much say in what happens to them. I believe that a huge advantage to developing a loving pedagogy is the way that it can empower children and enable them to feel less powerless. In adopting a loving pedagogy educators take time to become attuned to children and remain sensitive to their needs. This in turn enables children to feel understood and offers them agency and a voice. Thus feeling loved leads to feeling safe and secure which empowers children and enables them to be ready to learn and have higher levels of wellbeing.

Feeling loved → Empowered → Ready to learn

The balance of power between adults and children

The balance of power between adults and children in our settings is an interesting notion to discuss. Balance being the important word here, so it should not be about one dominating the other. Adults will always need to safeguard children, oversee them and act in their best interests because they are aware of the bigger picture and any consequences or implications that might arise from particular activities or behaviours in our settings. However, perhaps thinking in terms of power is misleading because it could imply winners and losers, powerful and not powerful, and that is not a helpful way to think about our relationships with children. Perhaps it is not necessarily about redressing the balance but more about empowering children, so that they are partners in the setting – not 'done unto' or bossed about, rather treated as equally as possible, offered choices, the ability to contribute to decisions that affect them and seen as competent in our eyes. If we view children as active, competent and powerful in their own right, with their own views, opinions, preferences and interests, we can ensure that we take these into account as much as possible and give them the tools they need to become more independent in the future.

An example of this is when we, as effective educators, bring ourselves physically down to children's level or lower when interacting with children, by kneeling or crouching down. This is an important way of levelling the power dynamic between the taller adult and the smaller child and an example of how adults can treat children as if they were equal in status. This also helps children to feel valued, which is part and parcel of a loving pedagogy. If children feel loved and valued, this will empower them to have self-confidence and to be competent learners. Thus, adopting a loving pedagogy is, in turn, empowering children as they feel valued and included while their interests are celebrated and accommodated.

We also need to empower children in relation to their emotional development. Young children are still learning what these big emotions are and have not yet mastered how to deal with them. We need to hold their emotions, be a co-regulator and role model how to cope with emotions ourselves, ensuring that the message that children receive loud and clear is that all emotions are acceptable.

Using a 'Head, Heart, Hands' approach, Judy's House Nursery

At Judy's House we are informed by attachment theory and use a reflective functioning strategy that we learned from Debi Maskell-Graham, which we believe empowers children called, 'Head, Heart, Hands'. This reminds us that learning is about what we know, feel and understand. It's also about children learning through doing and having adults who understand the child.

Head: Us as practitioners/parents focusing on the child and thinking about them – seeing the world through their eyes.

Heart: Us as practitioners/parents putting ourselves inside the child and feeling their feelings – feeling what it is like for them.

Hands: Us as practitioners/parents doing and saying things to let the child know that we are trying to understand them – validating and valuing them.

We use this approach directly with the children as a way of supporting them emotionally, empathising and acknowledging their feelings. We use phrases such as, "I can see you might be feeling 'angry' or 'sad'" and give the child time to respond. Depending on the child and their response, we might then place our hands on their shoulders or give them a hug and allow the child to release the stress and anxiety they may have. However, we would always ask if it is ok to give them a hug or if they would prefer to talk from a distance.

Actively listening to children

When effective educators truly appreciate what children want and need, they will plan for this and children's needs will be supported. They will take into consideration children's views and offer them choices, helping them to be independent. Article 12 of the United Nations Convention on the Rights of the Child is regularly quoted in relation to children's right to be heard and is summarised as: "Every child has the right to express their views, feelings and wishes in all matters affecting them, and to have their views considered and taken seriously" (Unicef, 1989). The UK government ratified this convention, enshrining it to law a short time later and the convention has been adopted by 196 countries worldwide.

Many early childhood educators want to give their children a voice and listening to children has become a very popular notion within early childhood in the last 20 or so years. Mainstone-Cotton (2019:17) describes truly listening to young children as a, "two-way act of intent and purpose", moving beyond hearing words to responding to them. It might be helpful to think about how you hear different sounds and can tune into and out of some depending on where you are and the context you are in. For example, if you are sitting in your kitchen doing some paperwork and the fridge is humming, you probably do not even notice it and can tune out of the sound; but if someone were to comment on how loud your fridge is, you would immediately tune into the sound and notice it a lot more. Our brains are able to distinguish between sounds we hear and sounds we need to listen to.

The same is true for listening to children. Sometimes we can be so used to hearing our children's voices that they become a little like background noise and we forget to really listen to them. This is linked with attunement, discussed in Chapter 7, when we are actively listening we are able to not only tune into any words or sounds, but also to respond sensitively to the child's body language and way of being. In this way we are attempting to better understand our children. You may have come across the Mosaic Approach, a form of research using several methods to listen to young children, which seeks to see the world from a child's perspective (Clark and Moss, 2017). Underpinning this approach is the notion that young children are experts in their own lives and have a wealth of ideas and experiences that we, as adults, should value and seek to gather and understand.

There are various ways that we can demonstrate that we value the children we work with and actively listen to them. For example:

- Try to see the world from their perspective.

- Listen to their words.

- Notice their behaviour and actions.

- Interpret their facial expressions and body language.

- Act upon things that they say.

- Take their views into consideration.

- Plan with their interests and fascinations in mind.

- Include them in the conversation.

- Never talk to other adults over their head.

- Get down to their level.

- Mirror their actions or body language.

- Comment or provide a commentary about what they are doing.

- Observe them while playing alongside.

- Act as a co-player when invited to join their play.

One setting shared how they plan 'adventure time' for their key person groups every morning. This starts as a way of checking in on everyone and leads into child-initiated learning. Actively listening to the children and their ideas helps to shape the future provision and ensures that the opportunities presented to the children fit in with what the children have planned and want to do.

Adventure time, Denmead Infant School

We do various things in key groups, starting each morning by checking in on everyone. We also plan and review for 'adventure time', which is child-initiated learning time. After each adventure we review and talk about what the children have done and think together about what they might want to do tomorrow. From listening to the children we tweak the provision each day to make sure they are given opportunities to move their learning forward in a way they love! Involving them in this way has been very empowering for the children and helps me to scaffold their learning in a way that's right for each individual child.

When we really listen to young children we are seeking to view the world from their perspective and to do this, "requires skilled and flexible researchers and teachers, who watch and listen carefully whilst being mindful of their filtering/interpretive gazes" (Peters and Kelly, 2015: 13). We need to acknowledge our own thoughts that might influence our analysis of what we see. It is difficult to remain non-judgemental or impartial when observing children's play. We have our own views on what to do, how to do it and why things should be done in a particular way and it can be hard to let go of this and to see things from a child's eye view. Most of the time these filters do not get in the way too much, but occasionally we can get hung up on a particular aspect that drowns out the voice of the child.

An example of this is when I was researching my book *Observing and Developing Schematic Play* (Grimmer, 2017). One educator shared with me how she was really frustrated with a child in her reception class who was deliberately plugging the sinks with green paper towels. She tried rewards and sanctions but to no avail. It was only when she realised that the action could be schematic, that she tried a different approach and began exploring the notion of plugging holes, running water and the water going through a boundary (or not!). She offered the child other opportunities to investigate this, outside of the toilet sink area and invited the child to explore these ideas freely using an old sink and plug and the water tray. This educator managed to see the behaviour through the child's eyes and saw it for what it was – exploration and investigation, not misbehaviour. Peters and Kelly (2015) share that really listening to the child's voice takes time and patience and it is important for educators to find many different ways of hearing this to do so accurately and authentically. Using the Mosaic Approach mentioned above or reading about the many different ways of listening would be a great place to start (Clark, 2007).

Advocacy and agency

Offering children agency goes somewhat further than just listening to young children. Agency could be described as believing that children are competent and capable of initiating their own learning alongside enabling children to feel and believe that they can have an impact on their own lives. It is when article 12 is fully put into practice, rather than having lip service paid to it. As Gurdal and Sorbring state: "Defining children as agentic is to grant them a mind of their own and with their own will and thereby acknowledge their self-efficacy and personal control" (2019: 1). It is about children recognising that they have a voice and knowing that using it may result in action, so children are an active agent in their own experiences (Mashford-Scott and Church, 2011). And it is about adults being an advocate for children to ensure that they have a say and that their voice is heard and acted upon.

An example of this could be when we organise the learning environment in such a way that enables children to access resources without their needing to ask an adult. Through listening to children we can try to gather their views on the resources and experiences that they enjoy and want more access to and can then tailor our provision accordingly. By affording children agency we are handing the control over to them, allowing them to be independent and empowering them to feel listened to and valued. The more we do this, the more we become advocates for them, promote their needs and help their perspective to be seen.

This can be illustrated in the case study about Lexie. The learning environment and ethos in the classroom meant that Lexie knew in sharing her picture with the teacher that it would be valued. In fact, it was more than valued and within the classroom it was as if it went viral! *The Magic Button* became a magical doorway for many adventures and was a source of inspiration in the classroom for the best part of the school year. Lexie felt valued, her idea was shared with others, including the headteacher. Her creativity and magical thinking was celebrated and other children in the class would see, from this example, that their own ideas would also be treated in this way, affording them agency too.

Lexie's story, Denmead Infant School

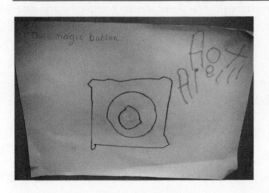

The Magic Button was created by Lexie and embraced by Rabbit Class. Lexie drew a button and told me it was magic. I stuck it on the wall and called it *The Magic Button*. A ripple went round the class and six months later we are still pressing *The Magic Button*! Anything can happen when you press *The Magic Button* from a new sound appearing to the head teacher popping in! Lexie's drawing could have gone in the bin and with it a way to engage and excite a class of reception children. *The Magic Button* is special to this class and unites us. It's only for us, it's special, it's ours and it helps build a classroom of love.

Markström and Halldén (2009) observed children in Swedish preschools and looked at their lived experiences of how they influenced and shaped interactions with adults and other children and therefore gained agency over themselves. They observed the children using a variety of strategies in order to manage their relationships with adults:

■ Silence – when children ignore the adult and keep quiet instead of responding, often the adult will give up trying to interact.

- Avoidance – when children actively avoid engaging with the adult, adults tend to interpret this as not giving assent and also give up trying to interact.

- Negotiating – when children bargain or negotiate to enable them to keep or regain control.

- Collaborating – when children rescue other children, for example by helping them or working together to do what an adult wants.

- Partial acceptance – when children defend their space, accepting in part the social order, yet still remaining autonomous and following the rules on their terms.

They conclude that children are active agents who have control and autonomy over their lives, which influences and shapes them on a daily basis. This fits neatly for me with the idea already discussed of children being seen as competent learners.

Self-efficacy

When we empower children we are contributing to their sense of self-efficacy, or their ability to believe in their own capabilities. This belief will have an impact on how children feel, think, behave and the way that they are able to motivate themselves. The term self-efficacy is usually attributed to Bandura (1994) and current ideas like growth mindset and positive learning dispositions like a 'can-do' attitude are built on this idea. Listed below are ways that we can help children to develop this sense.

- Offer opportunities where children can be successful in their learning – think 80 per cent can do, 20 per cent challenge.

- Encourage a 'can do' attitude using phrases like, "Let's try" and replace "I can't" statements with, "You can't ... yet!"

- Teach children that our brains can get stronger and will grow with us through our lives as we keep learning.

- Praise effort rather than attainment or accomplishments; for example "Wow, you must have spent a long time building that tall tower!"

- Label praise, giving children feedback on the great things they are doing: "Thank you for putting your coat on when I asked you to!"

- Always try to catch children trying to do the right thing rather than chastise for doing the wrong thing; for example "Sarah, I love how you are sharing the basket with Izzy – great job!"

- Notice when children are being persistent or persevering in their play and praise this; for example "You tried really hard to balance on the log and you got half way across, that's amazing!"

■ Talk about what to do when challenges arise and how we can keep going or get up brush ourselves down and try again.

■ Encourage children to see failing as a normal part of the journey to succeeding and role model resilience and bouncing back after difficulties; for example "Ok, that didn't work so I've learned not to do it that way again, what else can I try?"

■ Use language like, "… yet", "It's OK to get it wrong" and "We learn from mistakes".

■ Teach children that there are no limits to their capabilities – they can be whatever they want to be in life.

■ Encourage children to be proud of the effort they have put in as well as the product or accomplishment.

■ Foster and model a reflective attitude using phrases like, "I wonder what would happen if …?", "How can I make it even better?" and "What can we do to improve this next time?"

Noah's story, Denmead Infant School

Noah was a complex boy in my reception class. He was bright, articulate and imaginative but struggled to regulate his behaviour. Like many four-year-olds he had frantically charged behaviour and appeared almost ready to burst, rushing for the next thrill of excitement and always darting around the playground. He controlled play, leading others with his ideas but not really playing with them, and his interactions were often interpreted by other children as hurtful or unkind.

As his teacher I needed to understand him better in order to fully support him. After some research and trial and error I realised much of Noah's behaviour was related to his underdeveloped proprioceptive system.* We put strategies in place to support this including heavy work and calming-down techniques. For example, we noticed that physical touch would help him to focus. He often needed his back stroking to help him listen and pay attention during whole class times. This physical touch helped him know where his body was so he could focus on learning. But more than this, he knew we cared for him deeply. He knew that when he came to school he would be greeted with a genuine smile. He knew that we would listen when he talked and not assume he had been unkind because someone else said so. He knew that when he walked in the room the adult's eyes would light up to see him there. That's how much we valued him for who he was – right choices or wrong choices, we would always be there for him. He had to feel the love, to know he was safe and secure and that we would help him through all the wrong choices and unkind hands. He needed his teachers to know instinctively what he needed. Small things such as letting him get his coat first and having a special job, and pre-empting the times that he found difficult became second nature to the grown-ups around him. We focused on what he was good at and supported his play and leadership skills. He bloomed under these circumstances. He was empowered to learn, to think about his actions and to know he had choices in his behaviour – which meant he was learning the skills to gain more control over this. He needed that loving relationship to empower him to be able to succeed in his first year at school.

* Proprioception is the sense that helps us to know where our body is in relation to the environment around us.

In the case study, Noah's teachers ensured that he felt valued despite sometimes making mistakes and empowered to develop his self-regulation skills. It would have been easy for them to assume, if a dispute happened, that Noah did it. However these educators did not stereotype him in this way. Instead they became advocates for him and gave him a voice, enabling him to feel understood instead of judged, which contributed to his self-efficacy. In addition, they loved him throughout, regardless of his behaviour, which links to my understanding of unconditional love.

Unconditional love

Thus, another facet of the empowerment of a loving pedagogy is the idea that our love is unconditional. This means that a child cannot do anything that will make us love them any less, or any more. They have not earned our love because of any attributes or actions. There are no limitations or conditions associated with our love and care and we are not loving them in order to benefit ourselves. For example, as a parent we would not dream of saying something to our own children like, "I'll love you more if you put your dirty clothes in the laundry" or "You can't have a cuddle until you've tidied your room!" We love our children regardless. The same should be true for the children in our care.

Unconditional love says:

■ We value and accept you for who you are.

■ We don't mind if you make mistakes.

■ Our love and affection is not earned.

■ You can't do anything that will stop us from caring for you.

■ We want to help you to be the best *you* that you can be.

■ Tomorrow is a fresh start.

Interestingly some people may confuse unconditional love with unconditional duty; for example, I have a duty to care for these children regardless of how they behave. However, unconditional love is a testament to the depth of feeling we have and the way we choose to act and react towards that child. From my own experience, I felt that my work with the children moved beyond just duty. And my love for the children in my care was not simply because I felt duty-bound to care for them; after all, I was paid to do it! My love was something that arose naturally and manifested itself in my relationship with those children.

I would be naive to think that everyone will feel this way. Not all practitioners working with young children or teaching within early childhood will feel the same as I do and, for some, my thoughts around a loving pedagogy may go too far, as discussed in Chapter 3. For others, they may equate this sense of duty with the type of love called 'pragma' (see Chapter 1) and see it as a valid representation of their love. However, children will learn that they are accepted for who they are and not judged for their behaviour or any other traits through being loved unconditionally.

Real love is a choice that we make – it is not reliant on feelings and it should remain constant regardless of our mood. Of course we can feel cross or upset with those we love, but love forgives and, most importantly, love heals the hurt. Think about a relationship between two adult partners. When I married my husband, I was attracted to him and I fell in love with him for who he was, but I choose to remain in love with him and to love him even though we are many years into our marriage! And he chooses to love me, even though he knows the truth about me, my bad habits and red-headed temper! This sort of love is not conditional, dependant on how we feel, or how we treat each other day to day; it is a constant underpinning love that says "I love you, warts and all!"

Eddie's story, Dandelions Day Nursery

Eddie is a very sociable little boy with a visual impairment. He loves being outside and is drawn to bright colours, light and moving objects, which are easier to see. When considering a setting for Eddie, his parents chose a nearby nursery where they already had a link with some of the staff, in the hope that this connection would help Eddie to settle in and be supported. Eddie's parents have been particularly impressed by different members of staff, like Nicki and Sarah, who have bonded with him on an emotional level. They have really learned how best to support him, valuing and accepting him as an individual, despite initial concerns about how hard it might be to meet his complex needs and loving him while offering the specific support he needed. In this series of photographs Eddie and Sarah were on a zoo trip. Sarah uses her deep emotional connection with Eddie

to help him to meet one of his most tricky targets in relation to his visual impairment – to track movement and to increase his length of vision to one metre – you can clearly see how he moves from looking directly at Sarah to tracking the movement of the penguin, sharing attention with Sarah. This really was a special moment and relied on the close relationship they had with each other.

While gathering the above case study, I was moved by a comment from the owner at Dandelion's Day Nursery who stated that that they are the lucky ones; through one-to-one work with Eddie they are privileged in getting to know him and his family so well. She said, "He is very loved by everyone in our setting actually and probably all down to his winning smile!" It is so important that we get to know children as individuals and ensure that any additional needs do not define the child. It is a bit like the familiar phrase, 'Label the behaviour, not the child'. Eddie is known and loved for being Eddie and that is enough. In fact, it is more than enough, because we want children to be themselves and a loving pedagogy accepts and values them because of who they are.

Led by the child

As mentioned in the introduction, the term 'pedagogy' refers to our leading the child and many early childhood educators would describe their practice as child-led. I was reflecting upon how we can also be physically led by children while researching for my Master's. In the narrative, Michael purposefully seeks out Heidi and leads her by the hand. Heidi demonstrates that she is happy to be led by smiling and following Michael while showing an interest in what he is showing her.

Michael's story, Widcome Acorns

Context: Outside area during free-play.

Michael (child) purposefully walks over to Heidi (adult), "Heidi, I want to show you what's in the tree stump!"

Michael takes Heidi by the hand and leads her off to the edge of the playground where the grass begins. There is a tree about one metre away and growing at its base are several green shoots.

Heidi smiles and says, "There's more over there too. We'll have to have a good look Michael. Do you know what they'll grow into?"

Michael answers, "Snowdrops?"

Heidi replies, "That's a good guess. We have snowdrops over there, don't we." She looks over to a clump of snowdrops in another area.

Michael uses the simple act of taking Heidi by the hand alongside his request for him to show her something. Through this non-verbal communication he demonstrates to Heidi that he is comfortable in her presence and wants her to follow him. Heidi takes his lead, follows him and engages in conversation about the plants that he has discovered in the garden. Through acting in a loving way Michael's voice is being heard, which is empowering him as it values his contribution. While reflecting on this observation, I considered where the power lay in the relationship. On this occasion, the power lay with Michael as he initiated the contact with Heidi and literally led her to where he wanted her to go. Heidi followed, yet not in a submissive way, but in a reciprocal way, her body language and conversation demonstrating that she was a willing participant. On further reflection, this scenario felt equal in terms of the balance of power. Equal because, although Michael clearly led Heidi away, Heidi reciprocates and points out some more flowers to Michael. She could easily have led him over to those flowers and it would have felt like a natural progression, without the balance of power shifting. Thus, for me, this was about a loving interaction and reciprocal relationship and demonstrates how easily we can allow ourselves to be led by the child. This links in with Chapman and Campbell's (2012) love language of 'quality time', when love can be expressed by spending time together and sharing moments. This idea was not will be discussed in Chapter 5.

For the purposes of my dissertation, I also interviewed three early childhood educators. In the interview, Heidi commented:

> I think they can only have that sense of security by having the love and foundation – the loving foundation – you know and the secure base that they've come from and they know that we're ready to take them off to the next chapter of their lives.

In addition, she refers to wanting children to succeed and thus pitching activities at the right level to avoid disheartening failure and also to accepting every child whatever their ability and ensuring that adults remain non-judgemental in their interactions with children. In turn, this enables children to feel empowered and adds to the image of the child as being a competent learner.

Lucy, another early educator who I interviewed, refers to emotion coaching, when they support children to talk about their feelings and learn how to problem solve and resolve conflicts for themselves. She describes it as, "A cooperative approach to help them self-regulate their emotions so that they can deal with different situations." This links with the theme of empowering children as Heidi elaborates that emotion coaching is "giving them the tools" that they need for the future. In addition, when asked how Lucy would define a loving approach with children, she talks about catering "to those personalities so everyone feels included and can succeed." These ideas are further explored in the next chapter.

Love and philanthropy

In researching this book I came across an interesting article posing the question: "Are children as young as three years old capable of being philanthropists and if so, what would this look like?" (Armstrong, 2011: 43). Armstrong concludes with a resounding yes, describing young children as "competent, compassionate and intelligent individuals" (2011: 48). I would agree with this too, although having always associated philanthropy with money, I probably would not have used that term. Young children are remarkably capable and I have witnessed incredible acts of kindness and compassion over the years initiated by some of our youngest children. For example, when my youngest daughter was two years old, she noticed daddy changing out of his shirt and tie after work, and went to his cupboard and got him a t-shirt, telling him it was on his bed. I describe in chapter 10 of *Calling All Superheroes* (Grimmer, 2019) how my eldest daughter at four years old planned a cake sale in aid of the RSPB and Rockhopper penguins. Children often demonstrate kindness and love and you can probably think of your own examples when your children have done just this.

Elaine's story, childminder

A three-year-old I once cared for was playing with a doll, sat on the sofa, whispering and cooing to her 'baby', gently shushing, rocking and stroking its head. I watched this child and was just so touched by how gentle and nurturing she was. It was so lovely to watch. Being the youngest in her family, it just got me wondering whether she had seen this behaviour before. Then realisation dawned on me, I had recently had a new baby start at my setting a few weeks before who struggled to settle. Maybe this child had been watching me and was re-enacting what she saw? It was a huge revelation to me how much children observe everything and everyone around them and its impact on them and their behaviour. This made me reflect how displaying love and gentleness to others can instil a loving nature in children.

This also links with the idea, discussed more fully in the next chapter, about demonstrating love through holding other people in mind. Although this book is focusing primarily on how educators can develop a loving pedagogy, we must also consider how children become loving and caring themselves. This will be a knock-on effect of our pedagogy in action. The more loving our practice becomes, the more loving our children will become too.

Monty's story, Pebbles Childcare

Monty had been attending our small, family-like setting since he was nine months old, full time, five days a week. The summer before he was due to start school, his family finally had their application to emigrate to Australia approved.

Monty had had constant access to loving, nurturing childcare from an early age and the setting had become his home from home, with the practitioners like family members. Monty had forged deep friendships, whereby a number of the children became like his siblings and they looked out for each other, supported each other (and fought!) in the way that only siblings can, with an undeniable love for each other but a day-to-day frustration of having to share toys and follow each other's lead in games!

For any child, a move to Australia, is huge, especially at a time when your friends are preparing to start school and you are going through the transition process alongside them but facing a totally different prospect to them. This could cause significant distress or anxiety for anyone. However, because of the nature of our setting and the depth of the relationships we had developed with Monty over the years, we felt we were able to ease any potential anxiety or distress this move could cause and so we set about making his last weeks with us as enjoyable as we could.

Monty created a 'bucket list' of things he wanted to do or places he wanted to revisit as a result of previous adventures and experiences together and we managed to tick off every single one! Similarly, as his favourite things were eating meat and swimming, we hosted a 'BBQ pool party' for all his friends, past and present, and invited his family too, to celebrate his last-ever session with us.

The loving family-based relationship we developed with Monty allowed us to prepare him for the biggest transition of his life, without him even experiencing a shred of anxiety or fear, only a sense of excitement and adventure. We feel he was able to enjoy his last weeks with us, well informed and understanding the enormity of the move, without feeling sad or anxious, because of his trust and belief in us as, not only his childminders, but as wider extensions of his family. He trusted us to do what was right for him, and if we weren't scared, he wasn't scared and he was able to leave the comfort of a family home that he'd grown up in for over four and a half years, and travel to the other side of the world and start a brand new school in a brand new country; a confident, happy boy with a sense of adventure and security that most adults would envy.

Before his departure, we created a book of memories and photographs of the years Monty spent with us and the adventures he had, which, as you can see from the photo, he now reads at bedtime or when he feels he's missing us. Also, once the family arrived in Australia, we had weekly FaceTime sessions and messages to his parents as we supported them during the house moves and transition to school.

Even to this day, Monty still calls and FaceTimes us to check in, catch up and share news, just as he does members of his family, which is a real testament to how empowering a loving pedagogy can be for the children in your setting.

In summary

Developing a loving pedagogy empowers children to feel safe, secure, valued, listened to and loved, which in turn enables them to become self-assured and confident. Listening to children and advocating for them offers them agency and affords them some degree of control. We should not view children as powerless, but instead as competent beings and co-players, equal in our interactions. Within this environment children will thrive, flourish and grow.

Questions for reflection

1. How can you ensure that you view children as competent and confident and offer them agency?

2. How do you ascertain the views of your children and see the world from their perspective?

3. What examples can you share of being an advocate for the children in your care?

References

Armstrong, V. (2011). Child philanthropy: empowering young children to make a difference *Canadian Children Directions and Connections, 36*(2), 43–48.

Bandura, A. (1994). Self-efficacy. In V. S. Ramachaudran (ed.), *Encyclopedia of Human Behavior*, vol 4. New York: Academic Press (pp. 71–81).

Chapman, G. and Campbell, R. (2012). *The 5 Love Languages of Children*. Chicago, IL: Northfield Publishing.

Clark, A. (2007). A hundred ways of listening: gathering children's perspectives of their early childhood environment. *Young Children, 62*(3), 76–81.

Clark, A. and Moss, P. (2017). *Listening to Young Children: A Guide to Understanding and Using the Mosaic Approach*. London: Jessica Kingsley Publishers.

Grimmer, T. (2017). *Observing and Developing Schematic Behaviour in Young Children: A Professional's Guide for Supporting Children's Learning, Play and Development*, London: Jessica Kingsley Publishers.

Grimmer, T. (2019). *Calling All Superheroes, Supporting and Developing Superhero Play in the Early Years,* London: Routledge.

Gurdal, S. and Sorbring, E. (2019). Children's agency in parent–child, teacher–pupil and peer relationship contexts. *International Journal of Qualitative Studies in Health and Well-being, 13*(1), 1–9.

Mainstone-Cotton, S. (2019). *Listening to Young Children in Early Years Settings: A Practical Guide,* London: Jessica Kingsley Publishers.

Markström, A. and Halldén, G. (2009). Children's strategies for agency in preschool *Children & Society,* 23, 112–122.

Mashford-Scott, A. and Church, A. (2011). Promoting children's agency in early childhood education, *Novitas-ROYAL (Research on Youth and Language), 5* (1), 15–38.

Peters, S. and Kelly, J. (2015). Exploring children's perspectives: multiple ways of seeing and knowing the child. *Waikato Journal of Education, Special 20th Anniversary Collection,* 13–22.

Unicef (1989). United Nations Convention on the Rights of the Child. Retrieved from www.unicef.org.uk/Documents/Publication-pdfs/UNCRC_PRESS200910web.pdf.

7 Holding children in mind

Introduction

When I first started thinking about what a loving pedagogy might look like, I found reflecting upon Read's notion (2014) of holding children in mind helpful, and it reminded me of how important it is for us as educators to respond sensitively to children and hold them and their individual circumstances in mind. This is part and parcel of a loving pedagogy, when educators think about children's needs, interests and capabilities and plan an effective environment and activities based around them.

This chapter explores these ideas and develops links with other ideas such as mindmindedness, attunement, empathy and theory of mind. It also considers our role as educators and how through developing a loving pedagogy we can support children through transitions and be more inclusive in our work.

Holding children in mind and attunement

When discussing intimacy and attunement, Read refers to educators' holding children in mind as they, "attune to their cues so their needs are met promptly and appropriately" (2014: 59). She explains that our understanding of children should be experienced by them as, "being loved and delighted in, for who you are, rather than for what you might be doing" (2014: 61). So children need to be accepted, warts and all! I would describe 'holding children in mind' as a loving pedagogy in action. It requires the adult to be available to the child, emotionally and physically, attentive to their needs and attuned to them. Read (2014) hints at this attention being unconditional and intrinsic rather than based on the child's attributes or abilities and offers practical ideas of how to do this, for example noticing that a child is wearing new shoes or asking about their visit to their grandparent's house.

Holding children in mind also overlaps with Noddings' concept of attentive love: "Attentive love listens, it is moved, it responds, and it monitors its own action in light of the response of the cared for" (Noddings, 2002: 136–137). As educators we are observing our children and responding sensitively to them in the moment. Both attentive love and holding in mind are examples of 'professional love', whereby an educator holds a child and who they are in mind, is attentive and responsive to their needs and considers how best to further support them.

During my own research I noted many times when adults took an interest in specific children and what they were doing or were playing with and then interacted sensitively with them. They were holding the children in mind as they remained attuned to their needs. For example, in both Kirsty and Jay's story, the adults noticed children on their own or looking slightly lost, and then gently intervened to check that these children were okay. Many adults may not have noticed these children as they were not upset or demanding attention in any way. However, in this study both Lucy and Diane noticed them and responded warmly, smiling and reassuring the children with their interested presence. This depicts 'holding children in mind' on a daily basis and demonstrates how we need to be attuned to children's emotional states as well as tuning in to what they are involved in and doing.

Kirsty's story, Widcome Acorns

In the outside area during free-play time, Kirsty (three years old) was wandering aimlessly through the playground, vaguely walking towards an educator, Lucy. Lucy immediately noticed Kirsty on her own, caught her eye and smiled at her while walking towards her. Kirsty smiled back as Lucy bent down and picked her up, lifting her above her head saying, "What are you doing, you little lovely?" Kirsty laughed and smiled. Lucy gently placed Kirsty back on the ground and both Lucy and Kirsty laughed together. Then Kirsty skipped off happily away from Lucy.

Jay's story, Widcome Acorns

Also in the outside area during free-play time, Jay (three years old) wandered along looking purpose-less. An educator, Diane, walked over to him, smiling and asked, "You OK Jay? You looked a bit lost then…" Jay smiled up at her and answered, "Yeah"

Diane asked, "Are you playing with Ryland?"

Jay nodded and said, "Yeah"

Diane smiled and said, "OK" As Jay ran off happily. She watched him run towards Ryland.

Milo's story, Widcome Acorns

During breakfast club, before the main session began, two children were sitting at a round table set for breakfast with a small jug of milk in the centre. Diane was sitting with them on a child-sized chair at their level and Lucy was preparing the breakfast in the kitchen next to them. Diane chatted with the children about their families asking Milo about his brother, Harry, who has left their setting to go to school.

"How is Harry getting on at school?"

Milo replied, "Harry's at big school"

Diane repeated this, "Yes, Harry is at big school. Does he like big school?"

Milo says, "Yes and I'm going to big school too."

Diane confirms this for him as she warmly smiles and says, "Yes, you're going to Harry's school in September, aren't you?"

So when educators hold children in mind, they tune into the children's needs, are sensitive, responsive and offer 'attentive love' (Noddings, 2002). Lucy recognises this as she reflects upon her practice in a discussion with me saying, "We're very inclusive and caring and will support a child if we think they're struggling." Educators at Widcome Acorns see acting in a loving way as a spectrum, from opening the door to a child and being pleased to see them to comforting them when they are upset and also enjoying their company and having a laugh with them. I observed such exchanges during my research period and concluded that these warm interactions were evidence that love exists within daily practices. The children were being held in mind; for example, adults would notice if a child was absent or arrived late or would complement a child's jumper or ask them about their older sibling or new baby at home.

An example of this was observed during breakfast club when Diane was chatting with the children at their level with an air of friendship and comfortableness, which reminded me of a group of friends chatting as they were waiting to be served in a restaurant. Page, Clare and Nutbrown (2013: 49) state: "Babies and young children need to feel accepted, liked and loved if they are to feel comfortable about themselves and what they can do." My observations at Widcome clearly showed that these children did, indeed, feel accepted, liked and loved. This observation was typical of many warm interactions observed in which the adults showed a genuine interest in the children's lives, in the same way that one would enquire about the family of a friend. Diane also repeats Milo's language back, which is another way of reassuring a child that you are listening to them, while demonstrating your interest in them.

Developing a loving pedagogy includes building close relationships and using knowledge of the children to plan effective learning opportunities. So holding children in mind is, in turn, empowering children as they feel valued and included. Their interests are celebrated and accommodated. Chapter 6 looks in more detail at empowerment and how a loving pedagogy affords children agency, helping their perspective to be seen and understood. This clearly links with the work of Meins (1997), who has coined the phrase 'mind-mindedness' to describe when an adult treats a young child as a being with a mind, rather than as a creature who just needs feeding and looking after. An example of this might be when a mother and baby are sharing a book and the baby points to a picture of a duck. The mother might respond, "It's a duck. Do you remember when we fed the ducks on the canal? Quack, quack!" This encourages the child to think and recognises that the baby has their own memories and needs to make meaning from the conversation.

Research has shown that adults who are mind-minded are more likely to have secure attachments with their children (Meins, 1998). When adults are mind-minded they are giving a clear message that they think of their children as individuals with their own desires, thoughts and intentions and, in doing so, they are helping children to develop theory of mind, which we discuss later in this chapter. For me, mind-mindedness links with attunement, when adults actively tune into the child and sensitively recognise children's cues, responding promptly and appropriately. According to Rose and Rogers, attunement is when a practitioner, "let's the child know his or her emotions are met with empathy, are accepted and (if appropriate) reciprocated" (2012: 41).

Ways that we can be attuned and hold children in mind include:

- Supporting the child in the moment, responding sensitively.

- Observing and noticing things they are interested in.

- Genuinely listening and acting upon what we hear.

- Co-constructing ideas during play.

- Being fascinated by what our children are doing and wanting to find out more.

- Considering the 100 languages of children.

- Using a Mosaic Approach to better understand our children.

- Interacting sensitively, with our focus on the child, not our agenda.

- Planning interventions for particular children.

- Providing specific resources based on our knowledge of the children.

Including everyone

Holding children in mind is particularly relevant when we support children with additional needs. It is vital that we plan around the strengths of a child as well as address their needs. We need to be attuned to them so that we can interact sensitively and respond appropriately. The case study about James is an example of how his educators wanted the very best for him and positively held him in mind.

James' story, Choo Choo's Nursery: visual timetable

James is a child on the autistic spectrum who attends our setting. From our observations, we noticed that he found transitions difficult in the setting, so we created a visual timetable for him to use during the day. We included basic symbols and the main elements of his day. We made the board portable, enabling it to be used in any area of the setting and personalised it  with photos of James eating lunch, painting and playing outside. James used the board to make connections between his day and the environment around him. We introduced him to the visual timetable one step at a time, initially putting the timetable at eye level in the main room that he likes to go into independently in order to allow him to explore the board. On the first morning James saw the board and walked over saying, "James, James, James". Once he acknowledged the board, we introduced the different transitions of his day using one or two words, while pointing at the symbols. We have repeated this several times when James has been interested in the board and have also started modelling to James how we can use the board by pegging up the different stages of his day and taking away each stage once it has been completed.

The practitioners involved in the day-to-day care of James took time to get to know him, to find out about his strengths and interests. They also observed him closely during sessions to identify when any tricky moments might arise. They noticed that periods of transition were particularly hard for James and, with this in mind, they created the visual timetable that supported him during the day. By holding James in mind and creating this specific resource they were trying to see the world through his eyes and adjust their practice to support him. Fisher states: "Only when we see the world through the child's eyes do we truly understand just what is involved in making adjustments" (2013: 166).

It is really important that we keep the child at the centre and consider their individual needs when planning provision, bearing in mind a child's age and stage of development, so it is difficult to generalise about what this support might look like. Despite this, there are some ideas that might be useful for all children, including those with additional needs or a disability, and help us to keep them in mind:

- Liaise closely with parents and carers, build strong relationships and get to know the child really well.

- Focus on the child's strengths and interests as well as any areas that might be of concern and have fair but high expectations of the child.

- Think about how we communicate through facial expression, gesture, body language, touch and spoken words with all children.

- Remember that behaviour is also a form of communication.

- Use sign language or Makaton to aid language and communication.

- Display a generic visual timetable at child height so that children can see it and use it during a session.

- Think about how we can use visual images or objects of reference during our sessions to enhance what we say.

- Use clear language and value all attempts at communication that the child makes.

- Ensure that children are aware that all feelings are acceptable while some behaviours might not be.

- Provide puppets or soft toy characters for children to play with and learn about feelings and emotions.

- Offer opportunities for role-play and for children to work together. We may need to teach children how to play and how to join in with each others' play.

- Ensure that the learning environment is adjusted to meet the needs of all children and any resources used reflect positive images of disability, ethnicity and gender.

- Provide opportunities for children to become more independent and take responsibility for their learning.

- Review practice as a staff team and reflect upon each child, sharing our experiences of how we have successfully supported them.

Being held in mind through transition

Holding children in mind does not stop when they leave our setting or our group. Although we understand that this is a professional relationship, as discussed in earlier chapters, we still have an emotional response. We often find that we think about our children from previous cohorts because, as Read points out, "Being held in mind goes on for a long time after the end of special relationships" (2014: 72). Even now, I find myself thinking about children I used to teach or care for as a childminder and wonder what they are doing now and work out how old they will be. I was recently out for a walk with a friend who used to teach in a local primary school and we met a young man in his 20s. He said, "Hello, Miss" and she realised she used to teach him. Thankfully she recognised him and even recalled his name. He was really pleased that she remembered him. This is reciprocal too. In Chapter 3 Lisa Gibbons talks about how her previous class call to her and she gets a 'flurry of hugs' if they pass in the corridor. And I have heard lots of stories from people who have fond memories of their early educators.

Graeme's story, Headington Quarry Foundation Stage School

I have found the more experienced you become the more naturally you can hold children in mind and have their best interests at heart. For example, we looked after a little boy, Graeme, who loved pandas. We had bamboo in the garden and he used to love bringing his panda in and we used to develop stories around it. When it came to say goodbye – I found a panda in the charity shop and gave it to him. That panda has become a significant part of his life as I found out recently. He is now in year 4 and his mum tells me his panda is still by his side.

Embracing a loving pedagogy will also ensure that we support children through a range of transitions, whether this is leaving a familiar setting or starting at a new setting and settling in. In fact, transitions are not only the move to a new phase of life but can also be about starting a new experience, moving from one room to another, changing from one part of the day to another, a sudden change in routine or unexpected event or changes in their home circumstances. As Daly, Byers and Taylor remind us: "Something adults may consider to be a small or insignificant event can be quite traumatic for children" (2004: 111). It is not the really big things that will always have the biggest impact on our children. It can be the small things, that feel really big for them, like having to go through a different door into their setting, or not being able to sit next to their friend today. So we need to see the world and our settings through our children's eyes to really try to understand how they will feel and what will affect them most.

Lisa Gibbons, Denmead Infant School: the girls' story

As an educator, have you ever wandered into a group of children's play, feeling ready to scaffold their learning, with a clear learning objective in mind, armed with some excellent ideas based around their interests, only to find they scatter in every direction to avoid you? This was me and a group of summer-born girls who wanted nothing more than to play dogs, cats and babies while playing on their iPhones (actually large cardboard dominoes they had repurposed). Despite numerous efforts since they began in my class, they didn't want me anywhere near their play, which was becoming an increasing problem. How could I move their learning forward through their play if they literally don't let me near them? In the end it came down to one thing; the relationship. It wasn't strong enough. They weren't ready to let me in and until they were I couldn't be as effective as I wanted to be. They were not children who were happy to engage with me because I'm their teacher and we hadn't yet built up rapport or trust. So one lunchtime I built a secret fairy den, with sparkly lights, cosy cushions, mini fairy dolls, pencils and notepads (all chosen specifically with them in mind). Four little faces peered into the classroom as I was putting it together. One of them couldn't resist and asked me what I was doing as they tiptoed closer. I told them I was building a special den for them, for us all to play in together. One girl said, 'For us?' and gave me the first of many hugs that year. In that moment I knew I had started to build the next layer in our relationship. The one that will allow me to teach them because they trusted me; they knew I cared about them and understood them as individuals and what they needed from me. This is what I now believe to be professional love and it is exactly what those girls needed.

Here are some ideas of how we can support children during horizontal transitions that happen during the day within our settings:

■ View transition times as part of the day, to be planned for and managed.

■ Give a warning to the children, for example "Five minutes until we tidy".

■ Use timers/sand-timers as visual aids to help demonstrate the passage of time.

■ Have a dependable routine and ensure that adults are consistent in their responses to children.

■ Offer incentives for children who might find transitions difficult, for example "Zara can choose the story today".

■ Use songs, rhymes, or chants, for example have a tidy-up song or a song that helps us to sit in a circle.

- Count down not up to a transition, as this ensures an end – counting up could go on infinitely.

- Pre-empt which children will find transitions difficult and offer them additional support.

- Use visual timetables and now/next cards as a visual reminder of the routine.

- Reflect upon all children and families and decide if they will need any additional support provided.

Becky's story, using a chatterbox

When Becky was due to begin in reception she was asked to create a 'chatterbox' with her parents at home. The idea was that she include some small toys and photos that are important to her. Then, within the first few days and weeks, the teacher and teaching assistants were able to have some 1:1 time with Becky and talk to her about her interests and the things she had included in the box. Children often become very animated when talking about their own things or things they have done. Becky remains quite quiet when talking to adults who she doesn't know very well, so using a chatterbox really supported her in her transition into school.

Here are some additional ideas of how we can try to make the transition into and out of our settings a smooth one:

- Build relationships with parents/previous settings/future schools.

- Consider children's holistic development, in particular their emotional needs.

- Share relevant information, for example 'all about me' type forms.

- Create chatterboxes or bring special things from home.

- Use transitional objects and comforters if needed.

- Share stories about transitions/photos/pictures.

- Engage in role play and puppets.

- Make changes gradually over time.

- Use home visits, settling-in sessions, transition meetings.

- Use high quality information (virtual tour, photos, website, prospectus).

- Communicate with all: children, families and staff – formal and informal opportunities to talk.

The role of the adult

One of my favourite images when thinking about our role as educators is described by Anning and Edwards.

> The role [of adults] is to open gateways to new understandings for children as they participate in the world around them. Opening gateways demands that adults journey alongside children and are themselves aware of the gateways and the opportunities that lie beyond them.
>
> (Anning and Edwards, 2006: 68)

This is such a lovely metaphor on so many levels. First, that we are journeying alongside the children and we can see the path they are taking and, second, that we can open the gateway to things that might be beyond our own reach. I imagine visiting some of my favourite beauty spots, where, from height, I can see for miles around and in my mind it is as if the adults and children were at the brow of a hill, looking through the gate, at the miles of stunning opportunities that await them where anything and everything is possible for them.

According to Fisher (2016) effective practitioners need to be: attentive, sensitive, responsive, respectful, genuine, a good role model and at ease in the company of children. This last point is quite important when we are thinking about developing our relationship with children. As adults, we hate it when it feels like someone really does not want us to be there or we pick up on an uncomfortable or awkward ambiance. If we are not at ease in the company of children and building genuine relationships with them, they will pick up on this and will feel uncomfortable themselves. When we enjoy the company of children and are excited about learning alongside them, it shows. Developing these bonds also helps us to hold children in mind as we are happy to think about them and their needs, as demonstrated in this example from College Green Nursery School.

M's story, College Green Nursery School

At College Green we write learning stories, which parents and carers love, and they really capture the relationship between educators and the child. We start with the child and follow up on interests. These pictures are an example of M's learning story. He was particularly interested in birds, so we gathered resources including a bird chart and binoculars and presented them to M as an opportunity to extend his thinking and learning. M loved it!

In Laura's story it is important to note how the voice of the child shines through. If children comment on appearance, like "She is pretty" or "He has black hair", it is important to accept these comments because they are the words of the children themselves and doing so validates their contribution. However, as a whole setting it would be helpful to talk about which attributes we might want to celebrate, for example character and kindness, because celebrating appearance can give children the wrong message.

Laura's story, Feniton Church of England Primary School

The 'special person' is chosen by the current special child of the week by pulling a name out of the 'special box'. This name is then stuck onto the child (which they wear very proudly!) to inform parents/carers that their child is the next 'special person'.

Parents have received a letter at the beginning of the school year so that they are prepared for what their child might bring in.

On the day of the 'special person', I invite the child to sit on the teacher's chair, where they can then inform their friends of three different things that they would like pictures of to go onto their poster. The children all go off and draw a small picture, before we all then gather and children can tell me why the child is 'special' to them. Ideas normally range from physical appearances to she is kind or she plays with me. I scribe these ideas, so I can later add a selection of them onto the poster.

Next, the child's parents/carers have also written a short paragraph as to why their child is special to them. I read this to the whole class. The child then has the opportunity to talk about photos that they have brought in to share with their friends. These are often family photos and the children love talking about what they have doing with their family.

They also bring in a couple of their favourite toys that they can talk about and we end the session by reading their 'favourite book' to the class that they have also brought in.

I then produce the poster for the child so that is ready for the following morning when the child comes to school. I have had parents from several years ago that tell me that their child has still got their 'special person poster' on the back of their bedroom door!

The whole experience is intended to be a celebration of that individual child and what makes them special and unique. It gives them an opportunity to talk about things that they are familiar with and confident talking about and even children who can be quieter on the carpet have come to life on this occasion!

One idea that helps us to consider the voice of the child is to write ourselves a note, as if it were from the children, about our interactions and think about how our setting might be experienced from the child's perspective. How does it feel to be loved in this setting? How do I know that I am loved? We can write positive messages and perhaps think about any times when our actions or words might have given a more negative message. These ideas can then act as a reminder of how to hold children in mind and the adult's role in this. For example,

- I like it when you sing to me or tell me stories, it makes me happy.

- When I am upset, using a calm and gentle tone of voice makes me feel that everything will be OK.

- I like it when you explain how you think I am feeling. Sometimes I am not sure what I am feeling because the big emotions overwhelm me.

- I don't like it when you talk to other adults in phrases that I cannot yet understand; it makes me feel left out.

- I like it when you kneel down and are on my level, smiling at me. I feel like we are best friends.

- I hate it when you are too busy to play with me. I think you are not my friend any more.

- I love it when you play with me. I feel very special.

- I don't like it when you say I can't have my favourite-coloured plate. I feel like you don't love me anymore.

- I love it when you give me a high five. I feel so excited I could burst.

- I love it when I sit on your lap for a story. I feel very safe.

Marlis Jurging-Coles, St John's Preschool: keyrings

In order to support our children, one of whom suffers extreme separation anxiety, we have created keyrings for them. Each family was asked to bring or send in photographs and we created photo-keyrings. The children can carry these with them throughout the day as a physical reminder of their connection with their loved ones without feeling overwhelmed or pressured. In addition, in some cases we have created a second keyring with a picture of the child, who

those in need can pass to their parent or carer in the morning as a physical act of separation with the attached promise that the keyring will be returned to them upon collection. This move has helped one child in particular who (despite never being forgotten) has a strong fear of being left and that his mother might forget to collect him.

Links with empathy and theory of mind

Holding the best interests of someone else in mind has a clear link to the feeling of empathy when we imagine how another person feels from their perspective. Shortly after my father passed away, my middle daughter at nearly four years old asked: "Is Granny alright now that Grandad is dead?" This is a very high level of understanding for a child so young because true empathy relies on our having developed a certain amount of theory of mind. Theory of mind is when we understand that other people have thoughts, feelings and beliefs that are different from our own. It begins to develop at a very young age when babies start to differentiate between animate and inanimate objects and interact with others more. It continues to develop throughout childhood as our understanding of social interaction gets more comprehensive. Most three-year-olds do not have theory of mind and would not be able to see things from someone else's perspective, whereas many five-year-olds and the majority of six-year-olds can. So at some point between the ages of three and six children develop this understanding.

Research that has assessed the level of children's theory of mind often uses a simple false belief test. An example of this would be if a child is given a box of chocolates and asked to open it. On opening they find that the chocolates have been replaced by cars. They are then asked if their friend, who is not here, were to come in and see the box of chocolates, what would they think is inside? Most three-year-olds would say cars because they are unable to predict what their friend would think and they know that cars are inside. However, if we play this game with a five-year-old, they would say that their friend would think there are chocolates in the box. They have successfully managed to look at the scenario from a different perspective and demonstrated theory of mind.

Theory of mind continues to develop throughout childhood and some experts have suggested into adulthood too. However, there are some groups of people who find theory of mind difficult, for example adults and children with specific needs such as those with autistic spectrum disorder (ASD), Asperger's syndrome (AS), major depressive disorder (MDD), mesial temporal lobe epilepsy (mTLE) or schizophrenia; deafness or hearing loss; damage to specific areas of the brain or people with specific language or social communication difficulties. Having limited theory of mind can make it very difficult to understand different perspectives or why people behave the way they do. It can also make a person vulnerable in the sense that they may not understand the true intentions of another person, which could become a safeguarding issue. Sometimes lack of theory of mind can also make it harder to engage in storytelling, take on a role in play or even to make friends.

Despite young children finding theory of mind difficult, many children will still be able to empathise to a greater or lesser extent. This is partly due to our ability to imitate others and mirror emotions from a young age. As research into neuroscience develops we are finding out more about the mirror neuron system (MNS) (Corradini and Antonietti, 2013). The MNS consists of brain cells in our pre-frontal cortex that fire up in response to our observing the behaviour of another person, helping us to imitate them or to work out how they are feeling. This has been likened to a virtual reality simulation in our minds of what an action or behaviour feels like (Ramachandran, 2009). It is not really a conscious understanding of the perspective of another but rather a natural and unconscious ability to empathise. An example of this is when a young baby cries in response to another baby crying or when we find ourselves laughing when in the company of others despite not hearing the punchline or joke. Our brain is able to mirror the feelings of others and enable us to emulate them.

Therefore, many young children will surprise us with their kindness and compassion, often demonstrating their ideas in actions, for example by caring for younger siblings or children in our setting.

Chloe Webster, Pebbles Childcare: baby W's story

Baby W is my daughter and the children have been part of her life forever, from my pregnancy, through to visiting me while I was on maternity leave and helping me set up her nursery, to her first visit to meet them all when she was six days old. They've formed an incredible bond with her so by the time she officially became a Pebble at five months old, they'd all been working on how to care for her and meet her needs and have always absolutely doted on her and wanted to be part of her care routine.

Theory of mind also involves complex language such as idioms, metaphors and sarcasm, which can usually be understood at around six or seven years old. This is why when an adult uses a phrase such as, "It's raining cats and dogs", we find our young children run to the window to look! As children get older they also become more socially competent, picking up on subtle social etiquette such as faux pas, which is when we 'put our foot in it'. An example is when five-year-old Lisa was given a present for her birthday from her Uncle John and she unwrapped the pink, sparkly tiara and wand set in front of him and shouted, "Urggh – I hate pink" and threw it onto the floor!

This is a classic example of faux pas and, as a grown-up, we inwardly cringe at this social mistake. However, at five years old, Lisa does not yet understand about other people's feelings and social etiquette. Children are learning from experience and from imitating others and thus they may learn the social rules prior to understanding why those rules are in place. For example, they may know that they are not supposed to point at the large lady sitting on the bus in front of them and comment on her size, long before they understand *why* they are not supposed to do this.

Generally speaking, understanding of faux pas does not develop until around nine to eleven years old. This is much older than we probably think and older than the age when an adult will brush away comments believing them to be cute rather than rude. However, although children may not have fully developed theory of mind, we can still support them in learning the rules about social interaction.

There are many reasons why we should support children in developing theory of mind. It helps them to self-regulate their emotions and teaches them a social language. It can also assist them to manage their own feelings and, in turn, move them from being egocentric to being more sensitive about how other people feel and to develop feelings of empathy.

Here are some ideas of activities to try which will support children with their theory of mind:

- Help children to recognise different facial expressions and follow eye gaze by playing 'hotter and colder' with facial expression and eye gaze to help child find a hidden toy.

- Teach children how to read non-verbal cues by over-emphasising body language and asking the children to guess the feeling.

- Play a 'guess the gesture' game or versions of charades encouraging children to work out feelings or messages relayed.

- Play the 'what if?' game, for example "What if I was singing loudly and mummy was trying to get my baby sister to sleep. What should I do?"

- Engage in pretend play, role-play and rehearse different social situations.

- Read stories and talk about what a character might do next, how they feel and what could happen, to help children to be aware that other people have their own thoughts and feelings.

- Plan activities that encourage children to think about feelings and emotions and what they mean.

- Tell jokes, use figurative language and idioms, explaining what you mean.

- Explain other people's behaviour in past, present and future scenarios.

- Use visual aids to support teaching about abstract concepts and sign language to aid communication.

- Consider different perspectives in games and stories.

- Write social stories (short description of situations, see example below) to help children to know what to expect in that situation (Gray, 2015).

- Use the language associated with thinking, feeling and believing; feel, forgot, think, know, guess, thought, believe, understand, excited, angry, sad, happy etc.

Sometimes I want to play with the same toy as my friend.

We may need to take turns to play.

Sometimes I have the toy first. Sometimes my friend has the toy first.

I always have a turn with the toy in the end.

When we have an understanding of the ages and stages of development relating to theory of mind, we can respond more appropriately to young children, understanding that sometimes the things they say are not unkind or rude. Instead they are demonstrating that they have not yet fully developed theory of mind.

In summary

Many early childhood settings already hold their children in mind and have an atmosphere of warmth, trust and mutual respect, where children and families feel welcome and have a sense of belonging. As I chat to educators and visit settings, I often witness warm and loving relationships and see environments planned around children and families. I meet adults who genuinely love the children in their care, build strong attachments and want the very best for them. They see the children and their needs as central to any decisions made in the whole establishment and children's ideas are listened to, strengths celebrated and interests accommodated. Holding children in mind in this way is a loving pedagogy in action.

Questions for reflection

1. What does 'holding children in mind' look like in your setting?

2. In what ways can you see your setting through your children's eyes?

3. How might you further develop children's theory of mind and empathy?

References

Anning, A. and Edwards, A. (2006). *Promoting Children's Learning from Birth to Five.* Maidenhead: Open University Press.

Corradini, A. and Antonietti, A. (2013). Mirror neurons and their function in cognitively understood empathy. *Consciousness and Cognition: An International Journal, 22*(3), 1152–1161.

Daly, M., Byers, E. and Taylor, W. (2004). *Early Years Management in Practice: A Handbook for Early Years Managers.* Oxford: Heinemann Educational Publishers.

Fisher, J. (2013). *Starting from the Child.* Maidenhead: Open University Press.

Fisher, J. (2016). *Interacting or Interfering? Improving Interactions in the Early Years.* Maidenhead: Open University Press.

Gray, C. (2015). *The New Social Story Book*, 15th anniversary edn. Arlington, TX: Future Horizons Firm.

Meins, E. (1997). *Security of Attachment and the Social Development of Cognition.* Hove: Psychology Press.

Meins, E. (1998). The effects of security of attachment and material attribution of meaning on children's linguistic acquisitional style. *Infant Behavior and Development 21* (2): 237–252.

Noddings, N. (2002). *Starting at Home: Caring and Social Policy.* London: University of California Press.

Page, J., Clare, A. and Nutbrown, C. (2013). *Working with Babies and Children from Birth to Three.* London: Sage.

Ramachandran, V. (2009) TEDIndia. Retrieved from www.ted.com/talks/vilayanur_ramachandran_the_neurons_that_shaped_civilization.

Read, V. (2014). *Developing Attachment in Early Years Settings: Nurturing Secure Relationships from Birth to Five Years,* 2nd edn. Abingdon: Routledge.

Rose, J. and Rogers, S. (2012). *The Role of the Adult in Early Years Settings.* Maidenhead: Open University Press.

8 Loving relationships

Introduction

A loving pedagogy is all about relationships: with the children of course, but also between the children themselves, relationships with parents, and any other professionals involved with our settings. It values staff and keeps wellbeing for all high on the agenda. This chapter will explore how relationships and connections underpin our settings and practice. It will consider the importance of attachment and think about how we can nurture the nurturers. Relationships are also considered in terms of creating nurturing spaces and working closely with parents and any other carers of the child.

Attachment

The importance of emotional attachments between educators and children is generally accepted (Bowlby, 1953; Elfer, 2011) and has been well documented with attachment theory now covered in most child development courses and qualifications. Children need to develop strong bonds with carers in order to feel safe and secure and we know that once they feel safe, they will be more ready to learn, explore and take risks. However, bonding with carers does not always happen naturally and educators need to be pro-active in enabling this attachment to form. Interestingly, the most important attachment figure to the child is not who meets their needs, like feeding them or changing their nappy, but instead it is the person who interacts socially, plays and communicates with them.

The way children are treated in our settings and the relationships that we develop with them within early childhood education has changed during my lifetime. Children are now viewed much more as independent, competent and unique beings who are each allowed an opinion rather than just a group of children who should do as they are told. Societal attitudes towards children have progressed and, in my view, become more accepting to behavioural difference and individuality. This is a very positive move and one that I wholeheartedly welcome. Young children are capable of making friends, having preferences, likes, dislikes and, as Chapter 6 discusses, should be empowered by our ethos and loving pedagogy.

Lisa Gibbons, Denmead Infant School: relationships

Relationships. A high level of trust, a bond, based on daily interactions that send a message of safety, of security, of understanding and of love. This is the key to everything I do as a teacher. If the relationship isn't there, then it's impossible to deeply engage with the children in my class. But this has been a gradual change in mindset for me. Fifteen years ago my PGCE training gave me little insight into building relationships with children and even told me not to hold hands with any children in my class. At 24 years old I didn't really question this and started my teaching career with this mindset. I think schools were very different at this time and the expectation to understand children and how to help them learn as individuals was not at the forefront. I think things slowly progressed and as I moved into teaching in the EYFS, where part of the curriculum is about building relationships, my mind set began to shift further and I began to be more and more aware of its importance.

For reception children, starting school is a huge step, where they have to build new relationships very quickly with adults and children in the setting. They are inexperienced at doing this and probably have spent most of their lives with familiar people. Even if they have attended nursery or pre-school it is probably a new experience, making new relationships, in a new environment. They have limited experience of relationships so it is our job to teach them.

I have seen a shift in the culture within my school, with lots of consideration and training from the local authority being given to help support teachers in understanding children's behaviour and in essence what they are telling us through that behaviour. Alongside this gradual shift my head teacher has very much driven this within my school and teachers are actively encouraged to think about children as individuals to support them in their development. This is not necessarily new thinking but the way in which we achieve this could be. My role as a teacher has evolved and now, more than ever, I am supporting families alongside their children – a role I do not see as onerous or 'more work'. In all my thinking around children and how best to help them achieve, flourish and be happy, I keep coming back to the same thing: relationships. If they are happy and secure then they will blossom.

The relationships I have with the children in my class are special, unique, and I feel hugely honoured to be able to experience this each and every day.

Although there have been critics of attachment theory over the years, as our understanding about neuroscience grows, the more it backs up our instinctive need to emotionally connect with others confirming attachment as a vital thread that impacts on our wellbeing. As Read confirms: "We now know due to advances and research on brain development that the key building blocks for emotional wellbeing, good mental health and future success in life are developed through close, loving and intimate relationships" (2014: 3). These strong attachments will lay the foundation for children to play, explore and be resilient learners and eventually more independent (Ebbeck et al., 2015).

Sally Kirkby, Headington Quarry Foundation Stage School: relationships

I develop a close relationship with my group because I have them all day. This also means that we can plan activities that can continue in the afternoon, like baking, and see the whole process through, not having to rush or wait until the next day. Sharing lunch together as a group every day on our own table is a calm, restful, nurturing experience. We get to chat about the lunch prior to going and the group supports each other in trying different foods. The children have lovely warm conversations around the table, with each other and with me, and the children enjoy having responsibilities of different jobs each day. I get to know the children really well and know their food likes and dislikes.

Continuing an idea or activity over the week is another thing that works well with having them all day. Sometimes children will bring in an object from home. This may end up being the topic of interest for the day … or week! One of my children would often bring in a transitional object. One day he brought in a huge cuddly shark. The whole group were amazed by it. My planning completely changed as the topic of conversation was completely shark related! The children's shark-related play extended into free flow where they spent the morning building a home for the shark with large blocks, they used cushions and blankets to make beds, the children became the 'shark family', at story time we all squeezed into the 'shark home' and I read a shark story, 'Shark in the Park'!

From their research Wilson-Ali, Barratt-Pugh and Knaus (2019) identified three key themes to be significant when considering how educators support adult–child relationships: dependency, planning for 1:1 time and self-settling. With regard to dependency, they found that 23 per cent of early childhood educators believed that the more a child was cuddled, the more dependent they would become (Wilson-Ali, Barratt-Pugh and Knaus, 2019: 226). However, several of these educators saw dependency as a positive and essential requirement of a relationship. Bowlby also saw dependency as a positive notion and one that leads to independence as the child grows older (1969). Planning for 1:1 time was an important aspect of building relationships and was particularly important during the settling-in period. Over 70 per cent of their research participants disagreed that children need to learn to self-settle when upset rather than be responded to by an adult (Wilson-Ali, Barratt-Pugh and Knaus, 2019: 226). This fits with current thinking that children need sensitive and fast responses from caregivers and should not be left to cry for any length of time in the hope that they will self-settle.

Lucy's story: ideas to help with attachment issues

The following ideas were presented to a parent whose child, Lucy, found separation very difficult.

- Draw a heart on your hand and the same on Lucy's hand and tell her that it's for her to think of you and you to think of her during the day.

- Give Lucy something that is precious to you (not too valuable in case it gets lost!) for her to look after and give back to you after school. It may reassure her that you're coming back because you'll not only want to collect her, but you'll also want the object.

- Make a photo keyring with a picture of you/both of you, which you can clip to her school clothes/bag or a lanyard she can wear around her neck.

- Give her a passport-sized picture of you to have in her pocket at all times and you can have one of her.

- Get one of those two half-heart necklaces for you both to wear (she might not be allowed to wear it in school).

- Get her teachers to create a visual timetable, if they haven't already, which clearly shows when you return to collect her, if possible with a picture of you.

- Have a routine that allows her to say, "See you later" (not "goodbye" – too final). Then perhaps have a big cuddle or a big kiss. She could wave to you from the classroom window; but remember that you would always need to wave back.

■ Pop a note in her lunch box saying see you very soon and telling her how much you love her.

■ Allow Lucy to have a dab of your perfume on her wrist or on a hankie so that she can also smell you and remember you at any time.

■ School needs to reassure her that it's ok to feel upset and miss mummy and that mummy misses Lucy too. But both mummy and Lucy need to still enjoy their day, otherwise it will make them sad. So they need to be able to remember each other and their love and look forward to seeing each other again.

Feedback from Lucy's mum shared that the hearts on wrists worked really well and her heart was the talk of the classroom! Lucy said lots of her friends pressed it as they were missing their mummy too. Now that Lucy is learning to read she is trialling the notes in her lunch box (see image in Chapter 5). They also wear the same perfume so we can smell like each other and remember each other if we feel sad! We plan to do the keyring idea next!

Ways we can help to build a strong bond and attachment with our children include:

■ Smiling and using positive body language.

■ Using the child's name.

■ Making eye contact.

■ Talking in a calm, soothing voice.

■ Using intonation (parentese).

■ Responding quickly and sensitively when the child is upset.

■ Becoming attuned to the child's cues.

■ Showing an interest in what the child is doing or interested in.

■ Spending 1:1 time with the child and providing undivided attention to them.

■ Informally chatting to the child during play and general routines.

■ Playing together and planning activities around the child's interests.

■ Explaining care routines to the child; for example, "We need to wash our hands now before lunch."

■ Offering labelled praise for the child's accomplishments.

■ Using physical touch, for example hugging, cuddling, sitting on lap.

■ Always responding when the child communicates with us.

■ Getting to know the child really well.

Page and Elfer (2013) highlight the emotional commitment of building strong attachments and the demands that these bonds can place on educators. We invest a great deal of emotion in the children we care for and developing these intimate attachments, when we often care for a number of different children at the same time, can be difficult. Some educators may even express concern about getting too close within a professional relationship. However, Page and Elfer see this strength of emotion as inevitable and, "not as an indication of professional or personal failure" (2013: 564). Many managers of settings may not have the capacity or knowledge of how to support their educators through the complexity of attachment in this challenging role.

Developing relationships with children whom we find it difficult to love

It would be naïve to suggest that love for all children will develop naturally and we will effortlessly love them all. As Chapter 2 has explored, a loving pedagogy is not an easy option! Just as we warm towards some adults more than others, we will naturally have some children who are easy to love and others for whom we find it more difficult. We should be honest about this. However, as we have discussed in Chapter 1, love is not simply a feeling or emotion; it is more about the way we interact, our actions and behaviour. Yes, feelings do come into it, but it is not the whole story. Therefore, I believe we can learn to love these children.

Julie Denton: finding connections

I'm very clear about the boundaries. If I have a child I'm finding it hard to connect with, I do a case study to think about why they are doing something to help me get to know them better. For example, if a child is annoying by making a whiny squeaky noise, it might end up being negative and become a barrier to our relationship. So examining why this child is acting in this way, and unpicking their intentions and behaviour, helps me to get closer to them, understand them, interpret and try to see how things are from their point of view. That strengthens the relationship and my connection with them in a reciprocal way. They know I'm interested in them and they feel that connection.

Chapter 6 explores the concept of loving children unconditionally. If we try to see the children we find it hard to love through their parents' eyes and with unconditional love, it might help us to see them as more endearing and loveable! Julie mentions that her strategy for overcoming a difficulty to connect with a specific child is to observe them more and try to interpret their behaviour, empathising with them. I think we have to consciously choose to hold these children in mind regularly and, in doing so, thinking about them will become habitual and familiar and will feel more comfortable longer term.

Biological parents do not have some sort of innate ability to love their children, although they perhaps have some preparation time during the pregnancy and some parents talk about falling in love with their child at birth. However, this is certainly not the case for everyone and many carers who are not the child's biological parent will love and treat the child much better than their blood relative. So we have established that love is not a magic power that naturally or supernaturally exists within a family. In fact, and sadly, research has shown that you are much more likely to be murdered by a member of your own family or close friend than a stranger! All parents and carers have to learn to love their children and their love grows deeper over time. And that is where love does carry a little magic – because the more loving our actions are, the more loving we will feel and we can never run out of love. Rebecca Brooks touches on this notion when she discusses loving children as a foster carer in Chapter 3. I heard a lovely anecdote, which is to imagine that the child is a seed that has come in a packet with no label. We need to offer the right environment, nutrients in the soil, water, pull out the weeds and then this little seed with grow, blossom and bloom!

Here are some ideas for how to love children whom we care for but might not even like:

■ Acknowledge that we are finding it difficult to love this child.

■ Hide any feelings of dislike or annoyance from the child and instead actively demon-strate that we like them through words and actions. Keep our own feelings in check. In my view this will become a self-fulfilling prophesy; if we pretend to like them, we eventually will!

■ Find out their interests and talk to them about the things they enjoy doing.

■ Plan to spend time with them focusing on an interest they have.

■ Try to work out their primary love language and then speak this language everyday.

■ Be committed to holding them in mind and consciously do this on a regular basis.

■ Try to understand any habits they might have that frustrate you and reimagine their weaknesses as strengths or assets. For example, if the child is very stubborn, see it as persistence!

■ Remember that all behaviour is communication, so ask, 'What is this child trying to communicate to me?'

■ Accept all emotions the child is feeling and use emotion coaching to support them.

■ Think of it as exercising our heart muscles by actively loving through actions and words and accepting that feelings are not the focus here.

Lucy Evershed, Bluecoat Nursery: Amy's story

When Amy started at nursery I began to get to know her and her family from a professional stance, as I was her key person. As always happens, very quickly I came to know her personality and interests and began to bond with her. Usually I find there is something about each of my key children that helps me start to build an attachment. This could be perhaps pretending to talk to each other on our 'banana phones' at opposite ends of the table at lunch club every day, or maybe the child wearing the same dressing-up clothes every morning and asking me to do up the zip and help put on the shoes. I think the bond becomes very strong once I tune into the way each individual child likes to interact with me, and how they prefer to receive attention from me.

In Amy's case it was through trying to reign in her low-level destruction of the nursery boundaries! For example, she would go into the toilets, turn on the tap, put her hands under the flow of water and angle them so the water bounced off them and flooded the cloakroom floor. She would also paint at the easel, but would also paint her own hands, arms and face as well as any

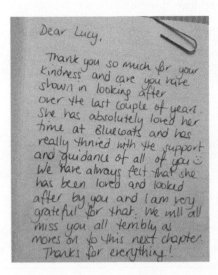

Dear Lucy,

Thank you so much for your kindness and care you have shown in looking after over the last couple of years. She has absolutely loved her time at Bluecoats and has really thrived with the support and guidance of all of you 😊 We have always felt that she has been loved and looked after by you and I am very grateful for that. We will all miss you all terribly as mores on to this next chapter. Thanks for everything!

accessible body parts of her friends; or tip out entire boxes of toys, pick the one item she wanted, then walk off leaving the rest on the floor. In beginning to gently teach her that this was not appropriate behaviour, she slowly began to respond to me and learn a little. She did not, however, take much notice of my colleagues when they tried to tame her high jinx, very much choosing to ignore their instructions. Maybe our bond grew deeper because she chose to listen to and respect me? Perhaps the way I spoke to her and how I was with her enabled her to build up trust and belief in me? As the two years went on, she and I chatted and played and, although I still quietly despaired of her antics, I also chuckled to myself at her sheer cheek and inventiveness.

When her parents wrote me a thank you card as she left us to go to school, they said they felt Amy "has been loved". This was the first time I had thought about my emotional attachment to her in this way. The way I feel about my key children is completely different to the way I feel about my own children, so I had never attributed this feeling to be one of 'love'. But after reading the note I realised that actually it was a form of love. This is how I could endlessly forgive Amy's behaviour and grimly look forward to each day she came into nursery. It was why I felt emotional on her last day and why, even now, several years later, I am still interested in hearing how she's getting on at school.

Holding the carers in mind

Veronica Read talks about the importance of nurturing the nurturers as she suggests that our role in settings also involves holding the absent mother in mind and taking care of her (2014). She is talking about educators being secondary attachment figures and the need to support parents, particularly at times of transition, departures or arrivals. As educators we need to greet parents warmly and sensitively, being aware of those parents who will 'drop and run' and others who will need our reassurance that their child will be alright. Many parents, even those who appear to be able to hand over their children easily, may be feeling anxiety at being separated from their child and worried if their child will cope with the day ahead. So we need to remain calm, reassuring and sensitive and try to treat each family according to their needs.

Parents may need to have the basics of attachment theory explained to them in terms of their child needing a secure base and building a close bond with them. We can suggest to parents that they try to have some 1:1 time with their child in the morning before they arrive at our setting or once they return home again. This will help them to re-establish their close bond and nurture their relationship.

In addition to parents, we are also nurturers, so we also need to be looked after and cared for. As mentioned earlier, being an early childhood educator is a demanding job – physically, mentally and emotionally – and we need to ensure that our setting and our colleagues can also support us in this role. Caring for very young children can be emotionally draining and, if we do not look after ourselves and our own mental health, we will not be in a good place to care for our children. Regular supervision can ensure that our own emotional needs are being met and can offer us an opportunity to talk about our key children if we have any concerns about our attachments with them. We must ensure that a professional dialogue about emotional attachments becomes a regular agenda item in supervision, just as safeguarding is. Read warns that if we, "do not receive and give ourselves as practitioners the support we require as carers then our ability to offer authentic love and care to those who seek care will be diminished" (2014: 1).

Julie Denton, caring for your own child or grandchild

I believe it's all about that emotion and connection – all the rest is much less relevant than the emotion you do it with and the relationship with the child and the deep understanding you can achieve from interpreting why children do what they do.

As a childminder, I have been looking after Mari, my granddaughter, which has made me think a lot about love and loving relationships. I would always describe what I feel for all the children in my care as love, but this has made me reflect upon whether this relationship is different or not to my relationship with the other children.

Interestingly, I have learned that because I love her I listen to her more and paid more attention to what she was telling me about the setting. I took more notice because I already had that relationship with her. For example, she wouldn't stay at the table when all the other children did and I suddenly became aware of the fact that she is so comfortable here, she feels like she can do her own thing. It's not naughtiness but a reflection of how comfortable she feels. So I reflected upon this and realised that the other children don't feel as comfortable and good in that environment. How can I make the children who aren't related to me as comfortable, as secure and as loved, as Mari?

I have discussed this during supervision with another practitioner and she explained that the relationship will be different when it's a child you're related to. However, sometimes our expectations for our own children or for relatives are different, often higher than for children in our care.

Developing a loving pedagogy is not necessarily an easy option but one that requires strength and boldness. As Freire (2005: 5) states, "It is impossible to teach without the courage to love." Adults naturally build close attachments when working with children and such relationships are risky. When children move on educators are at risk of feeling bereft. Thus courage is needed to allow these relationships to deepen and to continue to love them despite this.

Sally Kirkby, Headington Quarry Foundation Stage School

Saying goodbye at the end of the school year is the hardest part and it is heart-breaking to say goodbye to particular children. The lovely thing about Quarry is lots of the families stay in touch by coming back to see us. Also, each year they come to our Christmas Fair and every summer term (on a Saturday) we have a, 'Bring and Share Picnic Lunch' for our families, new and old, this is very popular and gets busier each year. It just feels like a big family.

Nurturing places

In addition to relationships with other people, we also have relationships with places and spaces as we make connections to the wider world. Part of developing a loving pedagogy will be endeavouring to create a feeling of love, an ambiance or sense of belonging and warmth in our settings. That will include in the space itself. While I was thinking about this, I began reflecting upon that well-known phrase, 'home is where the heart is'. And it is. I found this out the hard way after my first year at university because my parents had moved out of our family home during that year to a different county. At the beginning of the summer holidays I was adamant that I was returning to my home county, where I had lived for the past 18+ years, despite the fact that my parents were no longer there. I found somewhere to stay and got myself a part-time job. But I soon felt lonely and realised that it was not my home any more. That was the last time I spent my uni holidays in that county. Instead I chose to holiday back with my parents, albeit to a new county and an area where I did not know anyone. But it felt like home.

We want to give our children a real sense of 'coming home' when they return to our settings every day. We want them to feel like they belong and are comfortable and we want them to feel loved. Elaine talks about how revisiting a place brought back the feelings associated with the house, being accepted for who she was and a place where she felt she belonged – "just plain simple love and kindness". Would it not be amazing if the children in our care have similar feelings when they revisit our settings?

Elaine Brown, childminder: feeling love in a place, a simple childhood

I recently had the opportunity of revisiting my late grandparents' house, I last walked out of the front door of that house around 15 years ago when my dear nan passed away and it was sold. The house where she was born, my dad was born – the house that saw lives begin and some lives end. The house that protected and held the family together in tough times such as my grandad going to war, and the blitz that saw nearby houses obliterated by bombs. That wonderful house that had lots of love floating around and held so many magical memories for me growing up. Since revisiting my grandparents' house, I've been thinking a lot about how times have changed, how modern childhood is a rush, wanting too much, receiving too much, expecting too much. When I think about the time spent at my grandparents, it was simple, it was real, nothing fancy, no frills, just plain simple love and kindness. A place where there was a gentle rhythm to the day, where I could just be myself and felt true belonging. I will always cherish those memories and they will never leave me. They are embedded in my heart and soul, they are part of who I am. That simple 'feeling' of just being, of calmness, belonging and connection … children today need that ingrained in their hearts more than ever, they really do.

(You can read the full blog post at https://waterinmywellies.blogspot.com/2020/02/a-simple-childhood.html.)

Building relationships with parents and carers

Many early childhood educators do not see much of the parents of children in their care. However, they do spend a long time with the children themselves. We may not talk about love to the parents and each family will have their own culture determining how much they discuss loving relationships in the home. Despite this, we need to begin the dialogue and get talking about love, albeit sensitively.

Lisa Gibbons, Denmead Infant School: partnership with parents

I always try to build a relationship with the families in my class, not just with the children. They are part of a wider family unit and this helps me to understand my class better.

We sent home luggage labels and asked parents and carers to write on them their hopes and dreams for their child.

This display was created with the labels and reminded us all to follow our dreams.

When engaging parents we must, first and foremost, empathise and try to see their perspective. Building a strong relationship with families is part and parcel of a loving pedagogy, and parents need to trust us in the care of their children. We need to earn this trust by being honest, authentic and welcoming to all families, treating them with respect. Holding their child in mind and keeping them at the heart of our provision will also help us to demonstrate our ethos.

Sometimes parents want to seek reassurance from their children's educators that their child is loved and cared for, that they are being thought about, held in mind and their needs catered for. Parents often like to talk about their children, so asking all about them is a good place to start.

Here are a few ideas of how we can develop relationships with parents and carers and help them to support their children:

■ Use a Mosaic Approach: one size does not fit all.

■ Have an open-door policy and always make time for parents if they have any concerns.

■ Consider the way we engage families, for example Zoom, phone, email, face to face, texts, website, leaflets and so on, and find out the preferred means of communication for each family.

■ Provide key information in different formats or languages and ensure all information sent home is accessible to parents and carers of all backgrounds and needs.

■ Think about the 'unique family', just as you would the 'unique child'.

■ Ensure that time is built in during drop-off and pick-up times for communication.

■ Offer stay and play sessions for parents to attend with their children.

■ Invite parents to workshops, meetings and events and provide information about opportunities for learning at home.

■ Arrange home visits as part of settling-in procedures.

■ Share with parents how they can become co-regulators of their children's emotional states.

■ Ask parents all about their children in order to find out interests, likes, dislikes and ways that their child responds emotionally.

■ Respect parents and how they choose to respond to their child, while sharing how we respond in the setting to try to aid consistency between home and setting.

■ Involve parents in our setting by using their talents, experience and backgrounds to enhance our provision and children's learning.

Nurturing relationships between the children

When providers adopt a loving pedagogy, it is evident in more than just the policies. The ripples are felt throughout the whole setting. Love becomes contagious and transferable to others. When I was a newly qualified teacher, I had a copy of Alborough's (1991) famous poem 'The Smile' on my classroom door and I believe we could substitute the word 'smiling' for 'loving': *Loving is infectious, you can catch it like the flu ....* It really is true that the more we love and act in loving ways and the more loving our interactions become with others, the more they will respond lovingly back. A loving pedagogy becomes a lived experience for everyone involved in the setting.

We notice this in particular with the children and their relationships with each other. If we role model and talk about being good friends and actively teach children about loving and kind actions, we will see this demonstrated more and more in their own lives. We can also help children to think about if the words we use are loving and kind or unloving and unkind. I came across an acronym that people use when talking to others, which reminds us to choose our words wisely. It is THINK – is what you were going to say:

■ True

■ Helpful

■ Inspiring/Important

■ Necessary

■ Kind?

We can use ideas like this with the children as we encourage them to use kind and loving words. It may be a little difficult for very young children to grasp, but it might be a helpful way for them to begin to realise that their words have an impact on other people. This concept is hard to understand and links with the ideas discussed about theory of mind in Chapter 7.

Children developing friendships, Pebbles Childcare

We believe there are countless benefits for all children growing up in mixed age groups. The children can form deep long-lasting friendships with each other that remain beyond our setting. For example, M left us for school over three years ago now, and O has always grown up with M around (since she was around nine months old). And so she is always over the moon when they are in on the same day in the school holidays – this photo documents a beautiful moment between M and O on the day they were reunited in the holidays. O embraces M and says "I've miss you M, you're my best friend."

Ways we can support children to build relationships with each other and be good friends include:

- Create mini-me photo characters of all our children so that they can play with each other in small world play.

- Talk about the qualities of being a good friend who is kind and loving.

- Create friendship pictures where we celebrate being friends with each other.

- Invite children to draw pictures or make cards for each other.

- Create communication-friendly spaces in the environment by providing dens or spaces where children can chat or socialise.

- Include friendship stops in the playground as spaces where children can go if they want a friend to play with. Then ensure that these stops are monitored and children are reminded to look for friends at the stops.

- Share books about friendship or stories where a character has been a good friend.

- Plan specific activities that directly promote sharing skills, for example turn-taking games, group activities, art/craft when you need to share resources etc.

- Write a charter that promotes sharing and kind, loving actions.

- Plan opportunities for children to engage in cooperative play.

- Talk about our friends and why we like spending time with them.

- Role model being a good friend and act in loving ways.

- Explain that small actions might make a big difference for others, for example asking a friend to play if they are on their own or smiling at someone who feels very sad and asking if we can help.

- Role model being kind and helping other people, talking through what we are doing and why.

In addition to these ideas we can use the problem-solving approach to resolve any conflicts that arise between children. This links really well with emotion coaching strategies that were shared in Chapter 2 and helps to restore relationships as well as supports children to own their problems and resolve them amicably. The approach uses six steps and is based on High/Scope conflict resolution principles (HighScope Educational Research Foundation, 2020). It helps us to see a fight, argument or disagreement as a problem that can be solved. Through adopting this approach, children learn to resolve their own problems and disputes and will, over time, need less adult support. Children who learn these techniques at a young age become more resilient and better able to cope with conflict as adults.

The problem-solving approach to conflict resolution.	Example of using this approach in a setting:
	Hara and Jakub were in the outside area. Hara was playing in the mud kitchen, Jakub joined her and wanted the whisk. At that moment Hara also grabbed the whisk. Both children began a tug of war over the whisk and the argument escalated with Hara and Jakub shouting at each other. This attracted the attention of Katherine, an early childhood educator, who quickly walked over to the mud kitchen area.
Step 1. Approach calmly, stopping any hurtful actions or language	**Step 1. Approach calmly, stopping any hurtful actions or language** "Hey Hara and Jakub, what's going on? Remember to use kind hands…" Katherine crouched down next to the children and gently held the whisk. She did not ask the children to let go of the whisk.
Step 2. Acknowledge feelings	**Step 2. Acknowledge feelings** Katherine said, "Hara, you look very angry and Jakub, you look very cross too!"

| Step 3. Gather information | Step 3. Gather information
"What happened?" The children both tell Katherine that they both need the whisk to play with and the tug of war starts again. Katherine holds the whisk still, preventing it from flying out of everyone's hands and hurting anyone. "Let's hold the whisk together and talk." |
|---|---|
| Step 4. Restate the problem | Step 4. Restate the problem
Katherine explains, "It looks like we have a problem guys because we only have this one whisk and (counts) one, two, children want to play with it." |
| Step 5. Ask for ideas for solutions and choose one together | Step 5. Ask for ideas for solutions and choose one together
"What shall we do?" Several children have now begun to watch this interaction. Katherine asks them for ideas too. One child suggests that they buy a new whisk and Katherine agrees that this might help for the future, but it wouldn't solve the problem right now. Then Hara says, "I know! Maybe we can take it in turns to use the whisk?" Jakub agrees although they have another discussion about who will have it first. Another child suggests that if Jakub has it first Hara can help them to pick petals for the potion they are making. Thankfully both Hara and Jakub agree to this suggestion. |
| Step 6. Give follow-up support as needed | Step 6. Give follow-up support as needed
Katherine checks that both children are happy with the arrangement and then comes back to the area five minutes later to make sure that Hara gets her turn with the whisk. She says, "Well done guys, you solved the problem!" |

Adapted from: HighScope Educational Research Foundation (2020).

In summary

Adopting a loving pedagogy will ensure that children attending early childhood settings grow up feeling secure, loved and accepted. This approach dovetails nicely with attachment theory and what we know about how young children develop relationships. We have noted that this stance may not be the easiest to follow and there will be children whom we find it difficult to love, yet that does not mean it will be impossible to love them, we will just have to work harder at it.

A loving pedagogy can also assist us in nurturing our staff team and helping our own emotional buckets to be full. In doing so we will be able to devote energy to making our settings nurturing places where children feel welcome and loved. As White states, the "fundamental need, desire, hunger, longing and potential gift of every human is to love and be loved" (2008: 45). A loving pedagogy is about creating relationships and presenting each other with the gift of love. What better gift can we give our children and what better gift can we receive!

References

Alborough, J. (1991). *Shake Before Opening*. London: Hutchinson.

Bowlby, J. (1953). *Childcare and the Growth of Love*. London: Penguin books.

Bowlby, J. (1969). *Attachment and Loss: Volume 1. Attachment*. New York: Basic Books.

Ebbeck, M., Phoon, D., Tan-Chong, E., Tan, M. and Goh, M. (2015). A research study on secure attachment using the primary caregiving approach. *Early Childhood Education Journal*, 43(3), 233–240.

Elfer, P. (2011). *Key Persons in Early Years Settings and Primary Schools*. Routledge: Taylor & Francis Group.

Freire, P. (2005). *Teachers as Cultural Workers*. Cambridge, MA: Westview Press.

HighScope Educational Research Foundation (2020). *How Does High/Scope Help Children Learn How to Resolve Conflicts?* Retrieved from https://highscope.org/faq.

Page, J. and Elfer, P. (2013). The emotional complexity of attachment interactions in nursery. *European Early Childhood Education Research Journal, 21*(4), 553–567.

Read, V. (2014). *Developing Attachment in Early Years Settings: Nurturing Secure Relationships from Birth to Five Years,* 2nd edn. Abingdon: Routledge.

White, K. (2008). *The Growth of Love*. Abingdon: The Bible Reading Fellowship.

Wilson-Ali, N., Barratt-Pugh, C. and Knaus, M. (2019) Multiple perspectives on attachment theory: investigating educators' knowledge and understanding. *Australasian Journal of Early Childhood, 44*(3), 215–229.

9 Concluding thoughts

Introduction

In the past there has been very little research that considers what love means within an early childhood setting (Page, 2014; White, 2016) and if, indeed, love is an appropriate subject to discuss. However, in more recent years, mostly thanks to Page and colleagues, there has been a resurgence of research into love within early childhood settings. I see this as a very positive step in the right direction and one that will only help in my aim to get love more widely talked about and the practice in more settings based on a loving pedagogy.

Children deserve to be loved and to feel loved, and attending a loving setting will aid them to learn how to love others. We can assist them in providing them a loving foundation upon which they can grow and develop. If early childhood settings ensure that their policies and procedures are founded on loving pedagogical principles we will have offered our children the very best of starts in their young lives.

It is vital that love remains high on the early childhood agenda. However, it is difficult to be pragmatic about love as discussions are reliant on interpretation due to its subjective nature (Campbell-Barr, Georgeson and Varga, 2015). In addition, as discussed in Chapters 1 and 3, the concept of professional love lacks a formal definition or common understanding. This means that educators must reflect upon what is meant when such terms are used. We need to redefine love and own it within an early childhood context to make the term more acceptable and my writing is an attempt to begin the conversation.

Love embedded in practice

Readers of this book may have been thinking, 'Well, we already do all of this. Tamsin hasn't shared anything new here.' And I agree! In my view, professionals within early childhood settings are already demonstrating their love for the children they care for on a daily basis, through holding children in mind, acting in a kind and caring manner and genuinely wanting the best for them. I regularly hear educators saying that they love the children and love working with them. The experiences that these children have, the relationships that they build and the attentive love that they receive demonstrates the power of love and helps to develop them into loving citizens of the future.

So what this book is doing is packaging what educators already do in a new package that could be described as a loving pedagogy. In an early childhood setting, educators have traditionally been *in loco parentis*, having a duty of care for the children they look after and I have heard it said that loving interactions are just part of the statutory role of an educator – they are simply doing their job. However, the intensity of feeling expressed by the many educators I interviewed during my research implies that it is more than just a job or a role they take on. They have described the depth of feeling and how this impacts on their actions and interactions, which I have interpreted as evidence of a loving pedagogy in practice.

Kate Bate, nursery class teacher, Cinnamon Brow School Nursery

Our school has a strong, Christian ethos and we weave our school's Bible verse from Jeremiah 29 verse 11 into the very heart of our nursery. We believe that God has a good plan and hope for each one of us because he loves us and feel our loving pedagogy reflects this.

Our nursery ethos is built on the school's core values of hope, compassion, forgiveness, thankfulness, perseverance and respect. Our nursery logo reflects this hope through the colours of a rainbow.

We reassure parents and carers that their child is important to us and design all our activities to help develop each child's confidence, resilience, uniqueness and self-esteem. We believe all children are unique and special and learn in different ways. We design an active curriculum, learning through play and responding to each child's individual interests and learning needs.

Our welcome video for parents and carers states: "We look forward to welcoming your child to our happy and vibrant Nursery where your child will be nurtured and loved." We deliberately used the word 'loved' because we feel it captures our ethos and approach. We are proud to be part of a setting that intentionally seeks to love each child for the distinct individual they are.

Many of the case studies and observations shared in this book indicate care, intimacy and love and, in one sense, it does not matter what we call it or how we define it, provided it is there. Having said that, I believe it to be helpful to use the term 'loving' to accurately describe our interactions and we should not shy away from that. I want this book to be counter to the 'moral panic' that Piper and Smith (2003) have observed when educators are afraid of certain interactions due to fear around child protection and safeguarding. I believe that a loving pedagogy is an appropriate approach to adopt in our settings and we can stand firm knowing that it is right for young children. Page, Clare and Nutbrown outline the challenge for early childhood settings as needing to have in place the policies and procedures that safeguard and protect children, while affording "appropriate levels of intimacy, affection, and, some argue, love, from their key person" (2013: 120). It is vital that in order to meet the many regulations imposed upon us, we do not compromise our ethos and we continue to build warm and loving relationships with children.

Love and kindness display, North Bradley Primary School

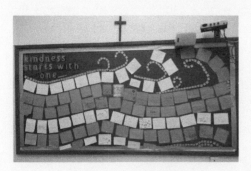

Recently our school introduced a new set of values. They are: love ourselves, love each other, love our world and love learning. We promote these with the children as much as we can and they reflect in our practice. We hope that everyone in our school community will support our values. So after introducing them, we invited each family to participate in a special homework over half term. We sent home a blue piece of paper to every child in the school and asked each family to record a way in which we can demonstrate kindness/love by writing an encouraging quote, song lyric, positive saying or random act of kindness on the paper. This display was the result.

In addition to quoting famous people, memes and songs, the children wrote things like: "Kindness is a gift everyone can afford to give", "Love is my family, my dog and my friends", "I love you to the moon and back", "In my family we always forgive each other when we have an argument" and "Do you want to play with me?"

The aim of this book is to inspire educators and to illuminate how love shines through the practices observed in many early childhood settings. Through sharing case studies, anecdotes, observations of adult–child interactions and having conversations with educators, I have highlighted how a loving pedagogy exists within day-to-day practices. Many educators demonstrate their affection for the children through eye contact, cuddles and touch, and in lots of settings this is encouraged both within policy and practice. These tactile interactions are evidence of love in action and help children to feel loved.

Developing a loving pedagogy also empowers children to feel safe, secure, valued, listened to and loved, which in turn enables them to become self-assured and confident. Children are not viewed as powerless but instead as competent beings, co-players and equal in their interactions with adults. In addition, many adults set up the environment in order to promote children's independence and empower them through encouraging them to problem solve for themselves and resolve conflicts.

Additional thoughts

Another issue that we may need to reflect upon in this day and age is the role of technology in our settings and how this could impact on relationships and professional love. Declan Nigel Dowkes, a student researcher at the Huddersfield Centre for Research in Education and Society (HudCRES), is researching this area and considering whether using formative assessment apps could enhance or hinder loving relationships. He reflects upon the potential barrier between adult and child that using a tablet such as an iPad could build, getting in the way of their relationship. It would be an interesting topic to reflect upon and to note whether using technology could damage relationships in our settings. At home, many parents interact with their children while their faces remain glued to a screen and I have even seen very young children and babies being pushed in a pram or buggy while their parent looks at their phone, rather than interacting with them. Should our settings set an example and avoid viewing children through a screen?

In conversation with Declan Nigel Dowkes

Do formative assessment apps create opportunities for meaningful 'professional love' interactions in early years settings or are they just an excuse for lazy caregiving?

In recent times, the way professionals aim to meet the individual needs of children has increasingly evolved. With a noticeable rise in expectations placed on early years educators from national government, it is not surprising that professionals are opting for time-saving and less stressful alternatives to meeting their planning and assessment obligations. As such, modern approaches to formative assessment, such as technology, is broadly viewed as a force for good. Despite being told that digital alternatives should not hinder practice, I take the view that, given the known detachment qualities of technology, there is a danger that such apps have the potential to form barriers between practitioners and young children that, in my view, should be avoided at all costs. Nevertheless, from my experience of visiting early years classrooms, formative assessment apps can indeed provide opportunities for children to take an active role in their learning and become engaged in the assessment process. This joint approach between infant and caregiver is a crucial part of how young children feel a sense of belonging, understand complex information and seek loving reassurances.

Lastly, I do believe that there is a place for the use of formative assessment technology within modern early years settings as the sector continues to navigate itself through an increasingly digital age. However, apps such as ones designed for conducting formative assessments, in my opinion, should be used in moderation to avoid ignoring the primary responsibility of early years practitioners, which is to place the individual care needs of each child at the forefront of every decision we make. With that in mind, I can only conclude by saying formative assessment technology may indeed make the daily tasks of practitioners easier in a very demanding profession, but this may prove to be at the cost of depriving children of quality intimate caregiving. The very thing the early years sector is known and admired for.

This book has mainly focused on relationships with people. However, children can also build very strong bonds with pets. Some childcare providers and schools have dogs or other animals who act as therapy pets to help children feel comfortable and less anxious. Research has shown that stroking a pet can reduce anxiety, blood pressure and have a calming effect for both the pet and the human (von Mohr, Kirsch and Fotopoulou, 2017).

The love of a pet, Pebbles Childcare

As much as we have become important figures in the children's lives and they seek physical comfort and contact from us, this has also extended to Billie the Beagle. The children have grown up with Billie and as such she is the most docile, affectionate dog there is. So many of our children enjoy spending time snuggling with her at points during the day, or actively seek her out for a cuddle and chat whenever they feel like they need or want to, as that is the relaxed, loving environment we have tried to create.

Three ideas going forward

Hopefully, this book has inspired educators to develop a loving pedagogy in their setting. So, if this is a new concept, then please read these three ideas of how to take this forward.

Firstly, as educators we need to be honest with ourselves and openly talk about love and loving the children in their care. Perhaps, you could hold a staff meeting where the main agenda item is love. Discuss things like: How does everyone feel about the term 'love'? Would we describe our setting as a loving setting where children feel loved? How do we know? Where is the evidence of a loving pedagogy in practice?

Secondly, we need to give ourselves permission to love the children in our care. We can do this by ensuring that professional love or a loving pedagogy is defined and described within our setting's policies.

Lastly, we need to ensure that a loving pedagogy, as defined by our setting, is totally embedded within our practice. So all stakeholders: staff, children, families, management committees, senior leaders and so on, are aware of and adhere to our ethos. So we need to be the adult we want our children to grow into!

In summary

Love can be observed within daily interactions; through positive touch, through an adult taking a keen interest in the life of a child or love can simply be observed within a smile. Early childhood educators often naturally build close bonds and feel a strong affection for the children in their care. They hold them in mind and are attuned to their needs and wants. I describe this as a loving pedagogy and one that all educators should aspire to as, within this approach, children will thrive and flourish.

Developing a loving pedagogy refers to caring for our children, thinking about and acting in the best interests of the child and developing a way of being that nurtures children within our ethos, environment, ways of teaching and interactions. Adopting this pedagogy underpins everything that a setting does, says and tries to be. This book has presented these ideas and argued that we need to have a foundation of love upon which our practice is based.

My parting wish for educators is that our current children and all future children in our care can look at our settings and say with confidence, like the little child from College Green Nursery School, "That's where love lives".

Additional questions for reflection

- How does the way you interact with children in your setting affect their positive relationships and self-esteem?

- Can love, feeling loved and being loving towards others affect children's cognitive development?

- Do educators feel able to demonstrate their love to the children in their care?

- How can educators demonstrate love in a professional capacity?

- What does a loving early years environment look like in practice?

- Can you work out the primary love languages for your key children?

- Could there be more than five love languages?

- What impact will understanding how children prefer to give and receive love have on attachment? How can you find this out?

- Can love be used as a tool to support children's behaviour? (In addition to the usual techniques that are embedded in best practice.)

- Do you have an ethos of permission with regard to acting in loving ways?

- Is it possible for an educator to pay lip service and follow a loving pedagogy while not actually loving the children? Would it even matter if the end result is that the children feel loved and are cared for appropriately?

- Does the whole practice of acting in a loving way create love?

- When loving children is a step too far for some educators, how can you enable them to feel comfortable with this approach?

- If educators are trying to remain slightly detached to make parting with their group easier at the end of the year, could this mean that the children's love for their educators is unrequited?

- What do you think about detached attachment?

- Where do care, love and intimacy begin and end? Do they fully or partially overlap?

- What is your first step in developing or further developing a loving pedagogy in your setting?

References

Campbell-Barr, V., Georgeson, J. and Varga, A. (2015). Developing professional early childhood educators in England and Hungary: where has all the love gone? *European Education, 47*, 311–330.

Page, J. (2014). Developing 'professional love' in early childhood settings. In L. Harrison and J. Sumsion (eds.), *Lived Spaces of Infant–Toddler Education and Care – Exploring Diverse Perspectives on Theory, Research, Practice and Policy.* Vol 11. International Perspectives on Early Childhood Education and Development Series. London, United Kingdom: Springer Publishing (pp. 119–130).

Page, J., Clare, A. and Nutbrown, C. (2013). *Working with Babies and Children from Birth to Three.* London: Sage.

Piper, H. and Smith, H. (2003). "Touch" in educational and child care settings: dilemmas and responses. *British Educational Research Journal, 29*(6), 879–894.

von Mohr, M., Kirsch, L.P. and Fotopoulou, A. (2017). The soothing function of touch: affective touch reduces feelings of social exclusion. *Scientific Reports* 7, 13516.

White, K. (2016). The growth of love. *Scottish Journal of Residential Child Care, 15*(3), 23–33.

Afterword

Demonstrating a loving pedagogy during a pandemic

Introduction

While writing this book the Covid-19 pandemic took hold of the world and everything changed. Therefore, this chapter is additional to the original plan. This is because I saw so many examples of a loving pedagogy in practice that it felt wrong not to write a little in relation to this and share these wonderful stories.

One of the strategies that many governments adopted to try to curb the transmission of the virus was to close schools and settings. In the UK, while educational establishments were asked to close to the majority of pupils, they stayed open for vulnerable or at-risk children and the children of key workers, adults whose roles were deemed necessary for the functioning of the country. Thus, many settings and schools were operating with a skeleton staff, with very few resources and literally living out their ethos.

I was encouraged to hear about beautiful and creative ways that settings were supporting the children, both during lockdown, when very few children attended settings and schools, and when these tight restrictions eased, allowing more children to attend schools and settings again. This chapter aims to document many of these stories as lived experiences within early childhood education. It will also reflect upon the opportunity now presented to the world to review how we view young children and the role of early childhood within society.

In crisis or a pivotal moment

I understand that the Chinese word for 'crisis' is 危机 which is made up of two characters: 危 meaning 'danger' and 机 meaning 'opportunity' or 'pivotal moment'. This is really interesting as it reminds us that every time we are in crisis there might be danger or scary times, but there is also an opportunity for us to review where we are going and the direction we are taking.

危机 (∧) For example, we could consider the ecological impact of human beings on the planet as nature breathed a sigh of relief during the pandemic, when there were very few flights, very little traffic on roads and less pollution. Organisations like Extinction Rebellion felt that our world was in crisis prior to the pandemic and we could argue that our planet has been presented with an opportunity and pivotal moment to change direction.

I also believe it to be the same for education. We are at crisis time, yes, but we need to see this as the opportunity it could be, for this pandemic to be a pivotal moment and a time when we take stock and change direction. For example, we can reflect upon issues such as testing and assessing young children. In the UK all statutory assessments were paused during the pandemic, which has meant that we are now lacking the data from several assessments undertaken on children under seven years old. This raises questions – will our schools still be able to teach effectively without the statutory assessment data? Will these children successfully continue in their education now that we cannot compare school's data? Will children still learn to read without having been tested on imaginary words in phonics? Of course the answer to these questions is yes! We already know that pigs do not get fatter by weighing them! This is an opportunity for us to change education for the better and remove any assessments that are not designed to inform us about children's learning and help them to make progress.

That is not to say that we should remove accountability measures. It is important that educators are held to account in relation to their provision for young children. Our children deserve to attend high quality settings, where their welfare is paramount and they are encouraged to be themselves and have no limits placed upon their learning capabilities. However, when assessments of children are used as accountability measures, this uses children's data inappropriately.

While reflecting upon this pivotal moment, I was inspired to read a new book edited by Cameron and Moss that damningly describes the early childhood education and care system in England as, "flawed and dysfunctional" (2020: 220). They explain that this is not due to the hard-working, often highly skilled and underpaid workforce, but that, "The failure lies with the system and the policies behind it, not with those who work in it" (Cameron and Moss, 2020: 221). They believe that it is time for transformative change within this sector and propose ten fundamental principles for a new structure within which early childhood education, incorporating care, could be delivered. They cover aspects such as having a phase of education from birth to six years which is free for parents and set up in a similar manner to maintained schools, well-paid maternity and parental leave and a graduate-led workforce that is well paid and has a status equivalent to current teachers among other things. I recommend reading this in full and it is available to download for free from UCL Press (www.uclpress.co.uk/products/128464).

Demonstration of love

As the world locked down and limited travel, families and friends had to find new and novel ways to remain in touch. We repeatedly used new phrases, for example, 'Can you hear me?' and 'I don't think you have your mic on.' Our common language now includes new words like 'lockdown', 'shielding', 'distancing' and 'support bubble'. We have even learned additional skills like reading books online and video-calling our friends for a virtual drinks party. Many families used conferencing software to remain in touch with other family members and grandparents and aunts and uncles found themselves reading live bedtime stories to the younger generation in a webinar-style manner!

Eliza and Katie's story: keeping in touch with grandparents

Prior to the pandemic we had moved to Scotland and our family remained in England. Eliza and Katie used to see their grandparents regularly until lockdown began. We had to find different ways of keeping in touch and taught their grandparents to use FaceTime, Messenger and emails. Granny Hazel even read some bedtime stories to them via the laptop!

Eliza and Katie are now so used to seeing their grandparents on screen, I'm not sure they'll know how to interact face to face! Although I know they can't wait for a big hug.

Fwd: Love

Dear Granny Hazel

I love you 😊.You are nice 👍.You have lots of poppy up things

.

Lots of love from Eliza 🖊🌼👀😹😄😎😀🙂📷🐬🏛🌐💨📁🦇 📠🐚🍞🥟🦴🔪🍤🍖🐚🍵🍊⏱💧👶🥐🥐⚡🔴🌙❄

Sent from my iPad

In the UK, and in other parts of the world, many initiatives began that aimed to keep people connected; for example, children were encouraged to draw rainbows and stick them in their windows. As a family we often went on local walks or cycles around the block nearest our home and my children enjoyed counting the rainbows we saw. It helped them to feel part of something bigger than just them and gave them a sense of purpose at a time that was unsettling and difficult. Social interaction is nigh on impossible when you are instructed to stay at home and save lives, so little initiatives like this made a huge difference.

In many parts of the world, people regularly congregated outside their homes, or leaned out of windows to applaud health workers and carers, who were putting their lives at risk on a daily basis to help others. Again, this helped to build a sense of togetherness as people collectively waved, cheered, clapped and played instruments, albeit from their own doorsteps or open windows. Our family live on a busy trunk road, so we decided to paint a thank you message and a large rainbow on our garage door. Other people did similar things and as a family we enjoyed looking for these thank you messages, which were displayed in windows, on flags, banners, posters and even on the sides of lorries. I heard about people leaving thank you notes on bins for the refuse collectors to find while others posted notes through letterboxes offering to do shopping or run errands for neighbours who were shielding at home. A global pandemic really can bring out the best in people!

Loving within settings – the new PPE

So you might think that PPE stands for 'personal protective equipment' – but it could stand for a loving 'pedagogy, passion and ethos', which has been vital throughout the pandemic. Many schools and settings remained open in England for vulnerable and at-risk children and children of key workers. These providers had difficult decisions to make. What changes did they need to make to their routine to enable children to stay safe? Did they need to alter their learning environment to meet the safety guidance or

restrictions imposed during the pandemic? How could they show love to the children in their care, while remaining more socially distant?

Bubble charters, College Green Nursery School

We are the only nursery school in the UK awarded the gold mark as a rights respecting school. We regularly create charters with the children, which are learning agreements that outline a code of conduct or agreed behaviours. The children have found this to be an invaluable strategy for learning and for resolving any difficulties they may face. Charters are a feature of our curriculum design and form the basis of our three termly learning themes of 'Know me before you teach me', 'Now you know me, where are we going?' and 'Enjoying one adventure and longing for the next.'

These images are an extract from our bubble charter, which we devised with children during the Coronavirus pandemic.

In every situation we face, we think how we can create and use a charter for this. When we were due to reopen the school, we wanted to make a child-friendly risk assessment, which helped the development of a charter to support

our children's well-being and their safety. We created a magical bubble charter that reassured children in a friendly supportive way. It also broke down the information to make it more manageable for them to understand. In the charter it explained about being in your own bubble and that we had bubble friends and waving friends, how to be safer at school and so on. We sent this to children before they returned. Also because of the nature of operating on a bubble system, the groups the children were in before had slightly changed. So we needed to reinvent ourselves and we asked the children to come up with some ideas for their new group name. Not surprisingly, name ideas were mainly around rainbows, sparkles, stars and love! But this in itself was reassuring as this was a reflection of what they associate their current situation with! Officially our children have named their bubbles: 'Zoom Zoom Love', 'The Sparkly Stars', 'The Sparkly Rainbows' and 'The Glowing Rainbow'.

Many settings held on to their loving pedagogy when sometimes it felt that everything was stacked against them. It was their passion for doing what they so strongly believed in and having a loving ethos that underpinned all their practices and kept them afloat. This was certainly the case for St John's Pre-school, which chose to reopen, standing firm on their loving pedagogy.

Marlis Juerging-Coles, St John's Pre-school

When we re-opened our setting we wrote the following letter to accompany our risk assessment:

As promised, here is our risk assessment and agreement of trust ... BUT, before you dive into the fine print, let me say a few things ...

As we worked our way through the various guidance, suggestions, 'expert views' and restrictions in an effort to explore how to safely return amidst the coronavirus crisis, our hearts sank for a while. What the documents suggested, at least at first glance, sounded like the direct opposite of what we believe is right to enable children's well-being and development. As we wrote the risk assessment, reports reached us of Early Years settings and schools alike sadly banning cuddles and stripping bare their environments to comply with all the new requirements.

In the end, we stepped back completely. We came together and discussed what is at the heart of our setting (just ours because, as you will know already, one size doesn't fit all!) and how we can make this work whilst still delivering the sort of care we believe in. We made some difficult decisions, such as temporarily stopping Forest School whilst it is deemed unsafe to travel in close proximity together, and the setting your children will return to will, no doubt, have changed to some extent.

But know this:

- Empathy and a deep care for all of our families, our children and everyone's needs is not banned.
- Love for our Pre-School family and a love for curiosity is not banned.
- We will cuddle your children as much as we did before, whenever they need it.
- We will sit and read to them, support their investigations and prepare an inspiring environment.
- We will continue rooting for them and feel excited for every one of their little wins.

Yes, there will be vigorous hand washing and children will be involved in cleaning up after themselves … but that isn't new. We've always practised good hygiene and we have always empowered our children to be part of the process, whether that is play or chores. Yes, the practitioners will have to stay away from each other (social distance applies to adults only within our setting) – but they have always been busy getting involved with the children so there's no change there. Yes, there will be some changes to the resources we'll have available, but we've frequently introduced different resources before.

As a Pre-School, we chose to come back in a fashion that is as true to our ethos as we could make it. And we believe, as you will see from our risk assessment, that we will be able to do this in as safe a way as is possible. However, risks remain. I must be clear about that and, as such, we are reliant on your help … The only way we will be able to pull this off is if we all work together. So please, be thorough when you read the assessment and the agreement. Please keep us all safe by playing your part. Our Pre-School depends on it. If you have any questions at all, please get in touch. We cannot wait to have you back.

Stay safe and well,

The team at St John's Pre-School

The question of whether or not adults could get close to, or have physical contact with the children during the course of the day became a matter for debate and many settings changed their policy on touch. During a webinar that I presented in August 2020 on developing a loving pedagogy, I undertook a poll to find out how many educators present had changed their policies and I was pleased to find that 60 per cent of those who responded (there were over 350 people in attendance) had not changed their policies during this time.

The UK government acknowledged that young children were unable to socially distance themselves. However, the general rule was to keep away from others as much as possible. Yet, as discussed in Chapter 4, we know that touch is vitally important for young children and denying children this could be damaging to their emotional wellbeing and development. Settings with a loving PPE (pedagogy, passion and ethos), remained clear that if a child needed a cuddle they would never deny them this and would offer comfort and reassurance to children in their usual ways. They decided on principle that children needed hugs and cuddles and more nurture than ever during Covid-19. For these settings, having reflected upon the importance of touch helped them to stand firm on their loving pedagogy during a time of crisis.

Thus, the pandemic was also a time to reflect upon the role of touch, not only in our settings, but in our lives. Several research studies looked into affection deprivation or what happens if we are deprived of physical touch and contact, linking it to depression, anxiety and loneliness (Okruszek et al., 2020). In a newspaper article about his research, Professor McGlone, from Liverpool John Moores University states:

Physical touch moderates our stress and helps us feel contented. Going without may well impact on a person's resilience to stress … Brains are good, if they're lacking something, they'll tell you to take action … With the lack of social touch mandated by Covid-19, your brain may well be telling you that you desperately need a hug.

(Coffey, 2020)

David Wright, Paint Pots Nurseries: a trauma and attachment-aware approach

Paint Pots Nurseries, who have adopted a trauma and attachment-aware approach, chose to keep our policies the same during the pandemic and still cuddle children if they need it. We posted the following statement on Facebook: "A parent was concerned about our statement that we would cuddle children if they needed it so I wondered if others were confused about that too. Based on the science and the evidence of the very low risk to children, government guidance recognises that social distancing for individual early years babies and children is not possible and would be damaging to their emotional wellbeing. We believe it would not be appropriate or possible for nurseries to care for children without physical contact. What we are doing, as recommended, is to maintain small friendship groups to reduce the risk of children coming into contact with large numbers of children or adults. This is government guidance based on the science as we start to emerge from lockdown. We have worked this way within our own settings and have spoken to many settings nationally and none have reported outbreaks. We have considered the long term psychological damage to children and made our decision. We will continue to show affection to children that need it but keep our adults apart." We also sent out our risk assessment for parents to read.

We received some lovely responses of support from parents and carers, and a few are listed below:

"I want you to cuddle my child, after 10 weeks not at nursery a lot of children will need reassurance."

"I'm so thankful you guys can give my girl a cuddle when I'm not there to. ♥"

"I would have been more upset if you didn't. I love knowing that when my child is upset/unhappy he gets the support he needs. A 3 year old can't be consoled with words especially when sometimes they don't even understand why they are upset themselves ☹"

"Love and empathy are important to caring for such young children. Abstaining would only cause more distress at a time when children are already unsure of what's happening. Well done Paint Pots for standing up for what you know is right, and for explaining how you're minimising the risk of contagion."

"I would have been more concerned that a childcare provider 'wouldn't' cuddle a child that needed it. The thought of my child being hurt or sad and being told he can't have a cuddle ... that breaks my heart. We are so lucky to have such a fantastic nursery like yourselves ♥"

"I would be far more worried about someone caring for my baby, toddler or preschooler who didn't prioritise their emotional wellbeing."

"How could anyone not cuddle a child if they need it? The rejection, sadness, worry (many more emotions/feelings any child would feel) would be damaging ... You are all fantastic at PP.'

Children are remarkably resilient and also have a real understanding of how love can indeed conquer our fears. They often surprise us with their astute comments and wisdom. Sue Searson shared with me a lovely story about how she saw one of her nursery children while queuing for a supermarket during lockdown, and the little girl called to her, "I love you! When we get back together we can have a big hug!" Everyone in the queue was touched as she reassured Sue that they would be together again soon and everything would be OK because of their love for each other. Sue explained how this felt as if she had already received a hug!

Sally Kirkby, Headington Quarry Nursery School

Ella's story

During lockdown we continued to open for keyworker children and, due to the low numbers of children attending, used a different part of the nursery called the daycare room. Ella, one of my key children, told me: "I really miss the Bumblebee group, and I really miss the workshop." She had always enjoyed spending time in the workshop, often bringing in items to use, like different-sized boxes or stickers. So I decided to change our provision and turn the painting table into a version of 'the workshop'. When I suggested this, Ella's face lit up and she excitedly found objects that she could use. This 'workshop' has continued inside and outside too and is very popular with many children.

Other lockdown activities

We have also been doing regular Zoom group times each week where children and parents from each group are invited to join in. We let them know in advance what will happen – for example, story, activity and song. My colleagues and I have found these times very special and often very emotional moments.

As a team we have been using an online learning platform called 'Class Dojo', and as a whole team we put together a song, 'I can sing a Rainbow', and a story in which we all had parts. We had an overwhelmingly positive response to this, receiving comments like, "Rachel and I love this Quarry team", "She [my daughter] watched your Rainbow song about 50 times!" and, "We love you all at Quarry so much, thank you". On Class Dojo we post stories and try and link them to a theme, and I have been reading my groups' favourite stories and always mention the specific children who ask for that story regularly. I have also been sharing photos of my pets and what I have been doing at home, which my children have really enjoyed. We surveyed our families about how they felt about us using Dojo to keep in touch and received great feedback, for example,

"Keeping a real sense of community. It's so uplifting to still feel part of something".

"You always put the children first on an individual level".

"Making us feel we are not alone".

"Everything, you are all amazing!"

"Being kind and supportive, it's really great to know you're there if we need you."

The pandemic and lockdown in particular was a difficult time for many families. Some adults were unable to work or be paid and, sadly, many people were struggling to have enough food. Many educators found themselves involved with sending food parcels to families in need or arranging for them to receive vouchers for food through government schemes. I read about an assistant headteacher from Grimsby who walked over five miles per day delivering school meals to his school's vulnerable children.

In addition to basic provisions, many schools and settings also sent home learning packs or posted ideas of learning activities on their websites. Lots of early childhood educators read stories online to their children and thought up creative ways to stay in touch with them. Many staff recorded videos, songs or wrote messages to their children wishing them love and encouraging them to stay safe.

Hazel Adamson, Lechlade Little Learners

We took the difficult decision to temporarily close our setting for a short period during lockdown and tried to keep in touch with families throughout. We sent each child a little pocket hug which consisted of a wooden heart with "pocket hug" written on the front, a packet of sweets and a sunflower seed in a pouch. We included the text:

Just a little note to say,
We are missing you!
Plant your sunflower seed
And watch it grow!
We hope to see you soon.
Love Hazel, Kimmie, Jo,
Harriet, Kim & Emma
Xxx

I also gave my staff team certificates when we were due to open our setting again to help to keep their spirits up. It is really important that we think about the children's wellbeing and mental health, but we need to be strong and well enough in order to look after the children in the first place. So prioritising the wellbeing of our staff team was also really important.

Certificate of Caring

Awarded to

Kimmi

For showing great love, care, inspiration and dedication throughout this crisis and for keeping me sane throughout everything whilst also juggling family life

Thank you

The pandemic was also a time for educators to take stock of their own wellbeing and focus on themselves. As we have mentioned in previous chapters, a loving pedagogy also involves loving ourselves, because then we find ourselves in a better position to care for others. In my view educators either found themselves with plenty of time on their hands as their settings closed and they were having to stay at home, or almost the polar opposite to this, being busier than ever, remaining open with fewer staff and a lot more work to do. Those who remained at work talked about very long hours, excessive (although necessary) cleaning regimes and additional paperwork.

A time to take stock and reflect

For many educators the pandemic was a time to take stock and reflect upon their practice and early childhood education. Several settings closed and furloughed their staff, which enabled them to dedicate time to their professional development. I found myself moving to a virtual classroom for my students at university practically overnight. This necessitated my learning new skills, trying out different technologies and being creative about how to either replace group work and discussion or plan online provocations that would encourage personal reflection. I encouraged my students to reflect upon their experiences and have included some of their responses here.

Hannah Wittig, early years teacher: a reflection upon the reopening of educational settings after Covid-19

Children in nursery, primary and secondary schools have not been in an educational setting for several months due to the Coronavirus pandemic. It is uncertain how this will affect children's mental health. I have researched children's wellbeing upon their return to nursery and have found the following. With many new rules in place, regular circle time will be necessary as well as clear posters explaining the rules and their importance. Children will have a lot of new language to understand, including social distancing as well as new rules like washing hands regularly, not touching other children and invading personal space. This will be hard for young children who are usually very tactile. Children must be kept calm and, although they need to be aware of the new rules in place, they must not be scared by them – clear communication and careful choice of words/descriptions used to explain this will be key to supporting the children into their 'new normal' transition and the understanding of it. Many of the children will have siblings that they have been with during this period of lockdown, but many will have been alone. This will be a challenging reintegration for them. Children may need to build their confidence and resilience. Using social stories could help this as well as teaching and supporting the children in pairs or small groups and rewarding positive behaviour. Children have not been with their peers so a time of adjustment will be required, as children may feel overwhelmed by the interaction. Reduced timetables (as well as visual timetables) or short sessions as a starting point may help as well as times of mindful meditation. This technique is proven to reduce anxiety and can even help boost creativity and productivity. A child-friendly programme helps the children learn how to stay calm and focused, remain positive and improve decision-making skills.

Lorna Ferguson, early years teacher: a reflection upon the reopening of educational settings after Covid-19, written during the pandemic

My English setting was shut on Monday March 23, following direction from the government the previous week. With no children to look after, to observe and to support the development of, my practice drastically changed. I switched to creating and reading stories to share with the children and focussing on auditing nursery provision. While limiting my practice, I was aware that other nurseries were still operating but drastically differently. Those early years settings were open for children of key workers and vulnerable or at-risk children. I was relieved about this because I was worried about these children not having the reliability and safety net of their school. Indeed, the consequences of the pandemic may result in newly vulnerable children being undetected. With a genuine possibility of parents losing their jobs, there will be unprecedented economic hardship for some families within just a few short weeks. There will also be unprecedented stress for families (economic worries, family concerns, illnesses etc). I know that inequalities during a child's early development can emerge early and unless acted upon, will persist and widen, hampering children's development and potentially leading on to interventions at school. Quite possibly, this pandemic has caused children who were not previously considered 'vulnerable' to suddenly become vulnerable in a short span of time. I also know that the sudden lack of structure and routine of children's settings proved to be difficult for families. I have talked with parents whose young children did not fully understand – and how could they – why they would not see their friends or family and have to be suddenly cautious about touching etc.

I saw photos from around the world of other schools and settings opening up with children socially distancing in their drawn circles and many changes in place. In England, soft furnishing will be removed once settings reopen. I am well aware of children that take comfort from the soft pillows and fluffy blankets that our setting has. For me, I cannot quite envision my nursery setting in a post-lockdown world. It seems otherworldly to have early years settings not having comforts or particular toys such as the classic sandpit. Washing hands is another topic that I have reflected upon as this is an area that one of my key children struggles with. I can imagine how difficult it will be to communicate effectively with him about the importance of washing hands without causing any panic. I am aware that these reflections sound negative. However some good things have arisen from this unpredictable time. For example, children have the opportunity to learn from home and spend more time with family, when family time has often been squeezed out of their fast-paced lives. I was walking along my road the other day and I laughed out loud upon seeing an "OFSTED RATING: UNGRADABLE" sign in the window of a family home. This caused me to pause and reflect on how perhaps a break from the 'pressures' of school and education is a good thing. We can take time to look at the structure of UK education. I can focus on my own pedagogical practice and appreciate what aspects of education that can and cannot be done digitally. For example, I have been able to take advantage of technology and create exciting and fun videos that I would not have normally done. Children and parents can use my videos more than once. We can have time to reflect on what works and what doesn't work. It has been and will continue to be an uncertain time. Some early years settings will not recover, perhaps there will be changes to education in the UK. It will be interesting to see the short-term and long-term impact.

Many training providers also delivered webinars, virtual training and set up some online courses. I was involved in these aspects through my work as an independent consultant. It was strange delivering the equivalent to a key-note speech to a silent and faceless audience. Despite the lonely delivery, I really enjoyed receiving personal messages after the sessions from educators who had found the content interesting. The fact that so many people took the time to comment and send messages of support was really encouraging and one educator said it was the best virtual training she had ever attended!

I see the opportunity to reflect upon our practices as a really positive outcome from the pandemic. Prior to Covid-19, many people, including myself, were living in an unsustainable fast-paced life with a poor work–life balance. The pandemic stopped the world in its tracks and gave us back some time. Time to read, think, play with our children and keep in regular contact with our families. I found time to ring my mum everyday, which we both loved, and my husband and I began a regular Sunday night quiz with our friends.

College Green Nursery School

During the school closure we participated in training and watched various webinars around reopening and adapting the school curriculum. We describe our curriculum as magical and loving and were particularly inspired by Jan

Dubiel's talk about a 'healing curriculum'. We discussed as a team what kind of curriculum offer and approach we were going to have and adapted our curriculum mapping for the summer term to support the children back into school. We knew we wanted our children to know that any changes had made their school learning environment safer and we decided to use the word 'safer' with the children. We also wanted our curriculum to include a smooth transition, to offer nurturing support so that the children knew that their wellbeing was important to us.

As a school we plan in the moment, putting the child's voice at the heart of everything we do. This is now more relevant than ever. We continued to plan using the approach of observe and respond according to needs. We wanted to ensure that our planning conversations explored our successes and questioned if we noticed any signs of regression.

My guidance on demonstrating love during a pandemic

I felt compelled to offer guidance to educators during the pandemic about how they could continue to hold on to their loving pedagogy. With this in mind I created a series of leaflets to support educators, which were available via the website of Linden Early Years (www.lindenearlyyears.org). The following paragraphs sum up my advice.

My advice, firstly and most importantly, explained that children may feel very anxious about the many changes that had taken place during the pandemic and that their setting might look very different. I encouraged educators to welcome their children and try to keep things feeling as normal as possible, even though they might feel anxious about working themselves. As the UK guidance at time of writing did not specifically mention close contact and touch, I advised settings to do whatever they felt was appropriate and fitted within their ethos, while protecting the children and staff as much as possible. I suggested that risk assessments and information shared with parents were specific and explained things clearly, for example how nappies would be changed, if they would allow children to sit on laps for a story or how they would respond if a little one initiated a cuddle or fell over and hurt themselves.

I also shared a few ideas about love languages (see Chapter 5) and explained we all love and feel loved in different ways (Chapman and Campbell, 2012). For example, some people feel loved if they are given a gift, while others will always want to hug those they love. During the pandemic, it was important to think about how children felt loved so that we could still demonstrate this love. Some educators may have needed to think of alternatives to a hug or a cuddle that were more appropriate, for example offering a gentle squeeze to a shoulder or having a fun elbow bump together! However, I suggested that there would still be times when it would be appropriate for close physical contact and advised educators to carefully follow their setting's policies and usual strict hygiene and hand-washing principles while still giving the children the close comfort they needed. I also reminded educators there are many ways that we can demonstrate our love without necessarily getting too close; for example, through keeping children's best interests at heart and holding them in mind in addition to building positive relationships and secure attachments with them; building nurture times into our routine, when children can refuel emotionally and we can take a genuine interest in their lives – by commenting on their tee-shirt or smile, for example!

Here is a list of the top tips that I shared with educators in the leaflet about how to demonstrate our love to young children during the pandemic:

- Read stories and books that include love, such as *While we can't hug* by Eoin MacLaughlin and *The Invisible String* by Patrice Karst.

- Use positive, affirming and encouraging language, for example labelled praise and words that build self-esteem.

- Listen to children, value their ideas and, whenever possible, act upon them.

- If your bubble can see another bubble of children, encourage socially distanced interaction such as waving, joining in with songs together, working on the same theme, playing instruments and even pulling funny faces at each other!

- Create mini-me photo people and give a set to each bubble so that they can still play with their friends.

- Take part in community initiatives, for example drawing a rainbow together and displaying it in your window.

- Play some music and dance together, copy each other's moves albeit from a distance!

- Create resources or plan activities with specific children in mind, reminding them they are special.

- Do something to help the children, for example finding their shoes, or the specific block they were looking for.

- Give children appropriate 'gifts', for example a daisy or special stone in the outside area.

- Help children to understand the concept of love, talking about people who love them and how to act in loving and caring ways.

- Role model acting in a loving and caring way ourselves.

- Make pictures for other people.

- Create letters and cards for others and send them in the post.

- Video call members of staff and children who are still shielding or who have not yet returned to our settings.

- Lastly, have fun together and enjoy each other's company!

Playful interactions

Children often engage in play that reflects real life where they recreate events or situations they have experienced. We call this sociodramatic play and it usually includes imitation play and role play. So during the pandemic, it is not surprising that educators regularly witnessed children role-playing with narratives including the coronavirus. Children may have donned a face mask, pretended to be a healthcare worker, or someone who was sick.

Sociodramatic play is a really important way for children to play at real-life events without the real-life dangers or threats being present. It is an opportunity for children to experience and process the emotions involved in a safe environment. The adult can role model interactions or take on a specific role, demonstrating what that character might do or say. Sometimes children will be happy for the educator to participate in the play and extend the narrative, but sometimes our role is just to observe and perhaps to help provide props and resources. The best environments are initiated by the children and co-constructed with them, so that they develop naturally through the expansion of the play.

We have also seen children creating face masks for their toys to wear or making their toys wash their hands as part of a game. At one point, my own children created their own mini-versions of lockdown games for their 'Lottie' dolls to play as they replicated things we had done as a family. For example, they decorated  their doll's house with miniature VE day poppies and held a socially distanced party for them.

Paint Pots Nurseries

A talented grandmother, Louise Hill, kindly crocheted this beautiful teddy sporting a face mask using a pattern by Aidan Legasto and presented it to her granddaughter's preschool on reopening. It has now become a much loved member of the setting.

In summary

This pandemic has had a profound effect on education and the early childhood sector as a whole. It has had an impact on all of us – we have learned so much and grown through this difficult time. We will have developed resilience, the ability to think creatively, to reimagine a new and different world. We may have learned patience and gained a new understanding of the importance of human relationships and touch.

We have seen settings who have kept children at the centre and at the heart of their practice, knowing that, during such a difficult time, children will need as much love, support and attention as possible. So, by kind and caring actions, holding children in mind and wanting the best for those in their care, early years educators continued to demonstrate love during the pandemic. This loving pedagogy demonstrates love's power in children's lives helping them to overcome pandemics and grow into loving citizens of the future.

I hope that this afterword has shared a handful of the delightful stories about loving kindness that the pandemic brought out into the open and has given you the opportunity to reflect upon your own experiences during Covid-19. I also hope that, most importantly, it has challenged you to consider how you can use this time as a pivotal moment to transform education for the better and what your role would be within this.

References

Cameron, C. and Moss, P. (eds.) (2020). *Transforming Early Childhood in England: Towards a Democratic Education*. London: UCL Press. Retrieved from www.uclpress.co.uk/products/128464.

Chapman, G. and Campbell, R. (2012). *The 5 Love Languages of Children*. Chicago, IL: Northfield Publishing.

Coffey, H. (2020). Affection deprivation: what happens to our bodies when we go without touch? *Independent*, May 8. Retrieved from. www.independent.co.uk/life-style/touch-skin-hunger-hugs-coronavirus-lockdown-isolation-ctactile-afferent-nerve-a9501676.html.

Okruszek, L., Aniszewska-Stańczuk, A., Piejka, A., Wiśniewska, M. and Żurek, K., (2020). Safe but lonely? Loneliness, mental health symptoms and COVID-19. PsyArXiv. April 10. doi:10.31234/osf.io/9njps.

Index

*For Product Safety Concerns and Information please contact
our EU representative GPSR@taylorandfrancis.com Taylor & Francis
Verlag GmbH, Kaufingerstraße 24, 80331 München, Germany*

T - #0292 - 270225 - C202 - 246/174/9 - PB - 9780367902667 - Matt Lamination